Fireplaces
and Wood Stoves

Fireplaces
and Wood Stoves

HOW TO BUILD, BUY, INSTALL AND USE THEM

By M. E. Daniels

BOBBS-MERRILL

Indianapolis / New York

Copyright © 1977 by Marie E. Daniels

*All rights reserved including the right of reproduction
in whole or in part in any form*
Published by The Bobbs-Merrill Company, Inc.
Indianapolis/New York

Designed by Bernard Schleifer
Manufactured in the United States of America

FIRST PRINTING

Library of Congress Cataloging in Publication Data

Daniels, Marie E
   Fireplaces and Wood Stoves

   1. Fireplaces—Design and construction.
2. Space heaters.   3. Stoves. I. Title.
TH7425.D36   697'.1   76-26948
ISBN 0-672-52175-X

CONTENTS

I

All About Heating

1

OUT OF A SMOKY PAST

Over the centuries man has kept himself warm by some strange methods and often, even stranger fuels. Ancient Egyptians, having little wood, burned straw and the stubble left after harvesting. Shepherds in ages past burned, among other things, manure—the fuel always available to them. And, in some instances, our ancestors of long ago devised methods of keeping warm while using no fuel at all. Even into the early 19th century, the beds of the nobility of some lands were occasionally pre-warmed by human bed warmers. But Normandy's Renaissance lacemakers are credited with a much larger scale fuel-less heating arrangement that allowed them to work a night shift. With the consent of farmers, they sat through the night from dusk to dawn among the cows in dairy barns, enjoying the animal warmth as they worked. When the cows were put to pasture in the morning, it was quitting time for the lacemakers.

Where wood was plentiful, however, the log fire was the popular source of heat. But when it was first moved indoors, it had a tendency to be smoky, and for good reason.

Though it seems difficult to believe now, the first fireplaces went into operation long before the chimney was invented. So the fireplace was just what the word implies—a place for fire. In its earliest form it was simply an area of the earthen floor as far as possible from the household combustibles. Later, it was a flat stone slab, usually in the center of the room. It had no walled sides, back or top, and of course, no chimney. Whatever wood was available burned lustily on the open hearth with nothing to impede it, and the smoke billowed up to the peaked ceiling and out through an opening later called the smoke vent. This was often fitted with a pole-operated lid that could be opened from floor level when the fire was burning and closed when it wasn't burning. As time went by, the vent was topped by a little steeple-like structure with openings in its sides, called a "smoke louvre." This not only shielded the opening from rain and snow but added a decorative touch to the roof.

Smoky as it was, the system had the advantage of simplicity, and it provided ample room for members of the household

Fig. 1. Open hearth was a housekeeping problem, but efficient.

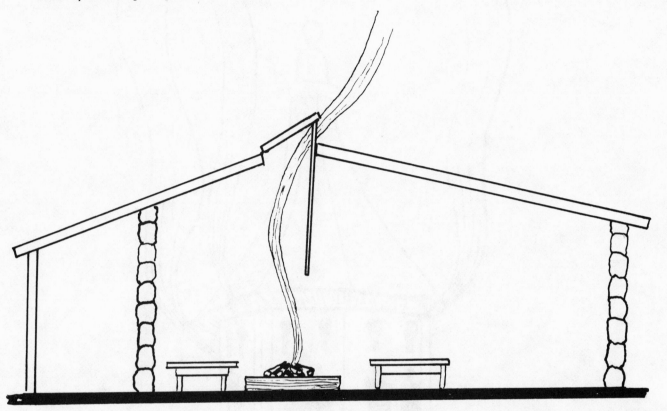

Fig. 2. Scandinavian home of the open hearth era, with roof vent and pole-operated vent lid.

to gather around the fire—all the way around it. Usually, too, there was more than the fire to watch. The andirons of the time, among the earliest of fireplace accessories, were forged with hooks or rings at graduated heights to support the ends of a spit on which the dinner roast could be turned. For more involved culinary efforts, an iron pot was suspended above the fire at a distance, by means of an adjustable support hanging from an overhead beam. Not surprisingly the open hearth served as a focal point of family life, which may in some measure account for the fact that our word "focus" is the Latin term for hearth.

One of the earliest fireplaces designed to heat a house without clouding the ceilings with smoke was the Norwegian "peis" (pronounced *pace),* now often the design basis for what we consider a strictly modern fireplace. As illustrated in Fig. 5, the peis was built in a corner of the room rather than in the center, with its hood supported by masonry walls, meeting at right angles. The post supporting the front corner of the hood in later versions was often an old gun barrel.

As the firewood was placed on end, leaning against the rear corner of the peis, wooden beams could be used for the sill

Fig. 3. A smoke louvre looked pretty on the rooftop and, in case of rain, saved the day for the housewife who might forget to shut the vent lid.

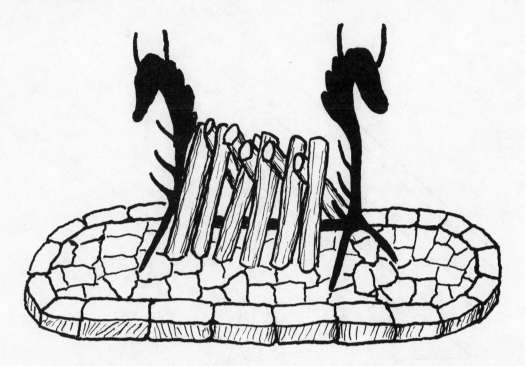

Fig. 4. Andirons were the same at both ends, with hooks to hold the spit that turned the roast—at the height the cook desired.

without too much likelihood of burning. And, of course, the smoke rose straight up inside the hood and out through the short, straight chimney, along with much of the heat. But the radiant heat from the fire was reflected into the room by the masonry walls. And, as the hood took on heat from the fire, it contributed some warmth to the room by heating the air in contact with it, and circulating it to a limited extent by natural convection. Often, too, the peis was built a short distance out from the corner walls of the room, sometimes allowing enough space to walk all the way around it. This boosted the heating power, as the vertical walls could then radiate heat into the room from the back as well as the front. The back of the walls added some convection heating to the room air, too. Even if

judged only by its reduction in room smoke, the peis was a sizable step in the right direction and a boon to housekeeping. So, though a major portion of its heat went up through the roof to the great outdoors, it worked well enough to survive for a matter of centuries.

Chimneys as we know them today began to appear during the 14th century on the castles and manor houses of the nobles. There, with wainscoting and tapestries to insulate the walls (which they did very poorly), the chimneys carried off the smoke from fireplaces built, in most cases, along the room walls rather than in corners. And, as with the peis, the rafters were no longer bathed by clouds of smoke—a situation that bothered a few scholars of the day. They feared the absence of the preservative effect

Out of a Smoky Past 13

Fig. 5. The peis was the first step toward ending the interior smoke problem. Logs burned on end in the corner.

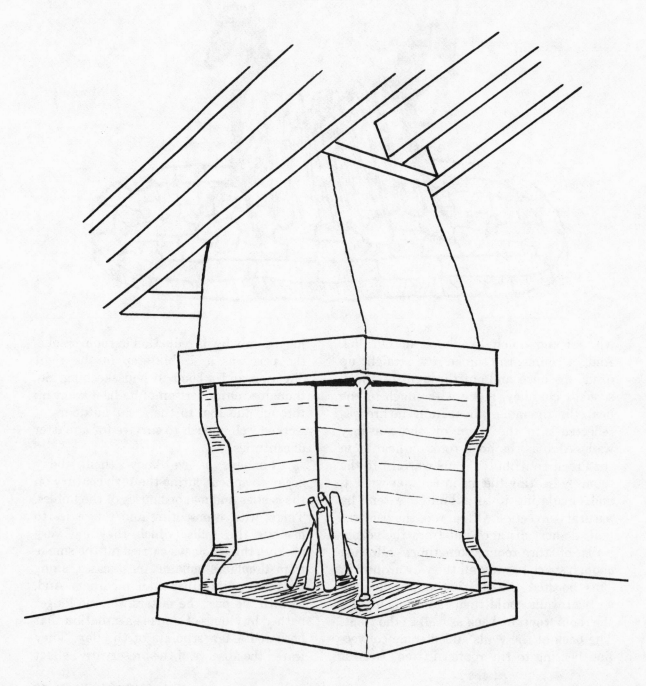

of smoke might cause the timbers to rot and crumble. But the real problem of the chimneys stemmed, instead, from their lusty performance. The great fireplaces of the baronial halls, with their massive and towering flues, burned logs at a furious rate that soon caused fuel shortages and resulted in firewood conservation laws. One such act was passed in England during the reign of Queen Elizabeth I. And the burning of coal, once a criminal offense, came into vogue.

But whatever the fuel, the generous proportions of the noblemen's fireplaces created still another problem. The surge of hot combustion gases and smoke up the myriad chimneys pulled such gales of air through the drafty castles that the nobles and their guests seated before the fire toasted their fronts while all but freezing their backs. To solve this problem, furniture had to be designed to block the tailwind. The wing chair, still popular today, is one example.

But despite its early drawbacks, the chimneyed fireplace was here to stay and destined for many refinements. The most important of these are to be found in

Fig. 6. When fireplaces moved to the wall they were often big enough to walk into and not too economical to operate.

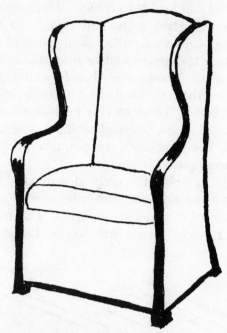

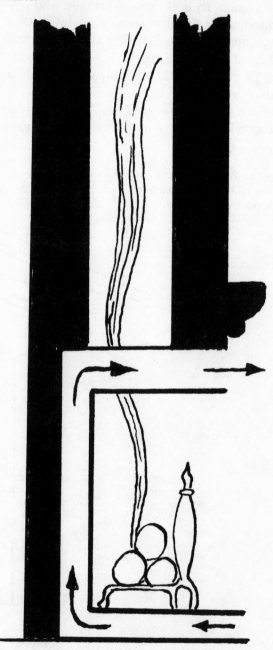

Fig. 7. *The wing chair, still with us today, was designed first to block the tailwind from giant fireplace drafts.*

Fig. 8. *The first circulating fireplace, by Dr. Savot, had ducts like this; it worked nicely in the Louvre Palace.*

today's fireplaces, if you know where to look. More about them later.

Many of these fireplace advances have been re-invented so many times over the intervening centuries that their actual origins have been lost in time. And some, considered relatively modern developments, really made their debut in the distant past. Circulating fireplaces like the trademarked Heatilator, for example, were in use more than 300 years ago. What is believed to be the first one was built into the Louvre Palace from a design by Dr. Louis Savot, a Paris physician born in 1579, who developed a penchant for more healthful conditions in the buildings of the day. Air entering openings near the bottom of the fireplace moved upward by natural convection (rising hot air) as it expanded with heat acquired in passing under the metal hearth and behind the metal back plate of the fire chamber before being discharged into the room through registers just under the mantel.

Later, the Gauger fireplace (named for another Frenchman) added a new touch to the idea by leading the circulating air in through ducts from outside, to combine ventilation with circulation. Gauger indirectly added a new word to the language—the word "ventilation" was first used in a translation of his writings on fireplace construction.

Although the ducting of outside air by Gauger's method never became widespread, the inside walls of his fireplace pioneered a principle still used in fireplaces, though in a simplified form. The Gauger fireplace walls were built in the form of an ellipse to reflect maximum heat into the room, much as the reflector in a spotlight reflects light. If you look at a modern fireplace you'll see that its inner walls are splayed outward, it is wider at the front, and its back is slanted from a point a little above the hearth. The flat, angled surfaces, easier to build than Gauger's ellipse, accomplish the same result of reflecting heat into the room along the most effective warming path. And they represent one of the many simplified innovations of an American fireplace pioneer whose career was even more interesting than his fireplace improvements.

This man, probably best known as Count Rumford, was born in 1753 in Woburn, Massachusetts, and began his career as Benjamin Thompson. That he was destined for scientific accomplishment might have been prophesied from his early years. At 14, his calculations of a lunar eclipse were accurate within four seconds. He was married five years later, a major in the New Hampshire Militia three years after that. Then, charged with being a Tory in the early days of the American Revolution, he fled to Boston, then to England where he became Under Secretary of State

for the Colonies. From there on his story seems almost fictional, as he was knighted by George III, and given leave by the British government to accept an offer from Prince Maximilian to enter the civil and military service of Bavaria, where he reorganized the army, trained thousands of beggars in useful work, and for a time was virtual ruler. Made a Count of the Holy Roman Empire for his accomplishments, he chose the title of Count Rumford from the name of his wife's home town, now Concord, New Hampshire.

His major contributions to fireplace design began in London around 1795 after his stint in Bavaria. According to his writings, his London work at one time brought more than 500 smoky chimneys under his care. But his notes also include designs for cooking appliances, kilns and furnaces. If his name has a familiar ring, it might stem from the fact that in the course of all this he also took time to found the Rumford Professorship at Harvard.

Probably the most important of his advances in fireplace design was the narrowing of the "throat" where the fireplace merges with the chimney, a feature that slowed excessive draft, reduced heat waste and greatly improved the room-warming capacity. This, plus the shallow hearth and reflective back angles used in his designs are among the features you'll find in today's fireplaces. And if you watch one being built, you'll see the "smoke shelf" that blocks downdrafts and falling soot—another improvement shown in his drawings.

The wood stove, however, was still to make its appearance, though efforts in that direction had already begun. In Germany, one fireplace with a metal plate in place of its rear brickwork heated two rooms, one on each side of the wall in which it was built.

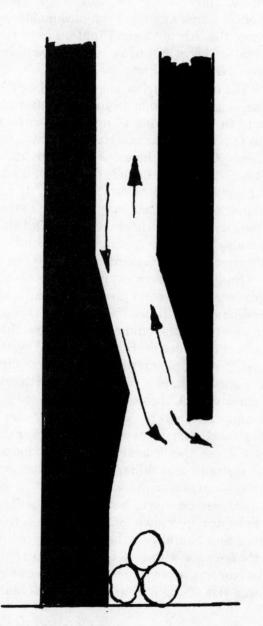

Fig. 9. Old style chimneys with no smoke shelf were prone to smoking because of downdrafts.

Fig. 10. Among his other developments, Count Rumford is credited with reshaping the fireplace to include the smoke shelf to catch soot and block smoke from puffing into the room. Damper (D) hinged to smoke shelf.

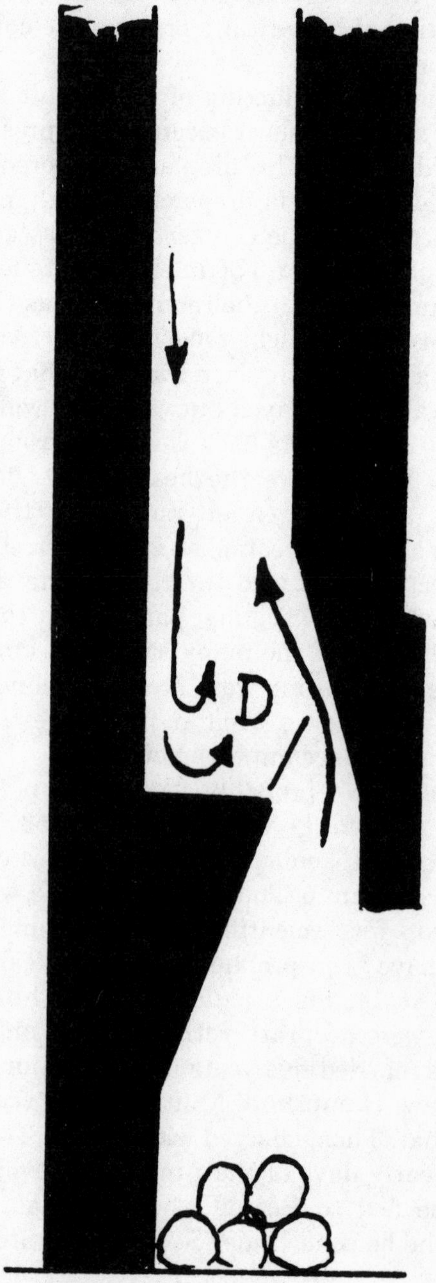

Heat from the metal plate not only radiated into the second room, but warmed the air and circulated it by natural convection, a method that was to enable the iron wood stove to revolutionize home heating. And long before that, Russian peasants slept atop their indoor ovens, warming themselves by the heat that passed through the oven's clay walls.

Ben Franklin's Pennsylvania Fireplace, described in a pamphlet sold in 1844, probably pinpoints the start of the wood stove era. It was a metal box-like unit set into a masonry wall. It not only radiated heat directly from the fire, but also through its hot metal front panel. And as the smoke and hot gases were routed through a circuitous path over a metal box behind the fire, air within the box was also heated and circulated into the room. In Franklin's words, "Your whole room is equally warmed, so that people need not crowd so close around the fire."

From there on, innovations came more rapidly in fireplaces and stoves, and combinations of the two. Today's Franklin stove, though quite different from the original design, is an offshoot that serves as a reminder of Franklin's contributions to our comfort. And the still familiar Dutch oven, in the form of a heavy cast-iron pot with a convex lid, remains a credit to Count Rumford who patented such a design. Although we use it today both as a stovetop and oven utensil, it was originally placed among the hot coals of the fireplace, often with a layer of coals on its iron lid. Today we can control its temperature without the skill required in Rumford's day and accomplish the same results with relative ease. If you'd like to try it, you can use it to bake yourself a loaf of soda bread from the following time-honored recipe that has been handed down for several generations. It may be varied by the addition of raisins, or a combination of raisins and caraway seeds, to suit your family's taste.

SODA BREAD BAKED IN THE FIREPLACE

Ingredients:
- 1 teaspoon baking soda
- 1 teaspoon salt
- 4 cups flour
- 1 to 1½ cups buttermilk

Method:
Sift dry ingredients together into a large bowl. Slowly add one cup of the buttermilk, stirring with a large fork. If dough remains too dry to gather into a ball, add the remaining buttermilk until dough is manageable. Pat dough out on a floured board until it is of a size you can place in your Dutch oven, roughly an 8″ round about 1½″ thick. Lightly butter the surface that will go on the bottom of the oven.

A precaution: Remove the Dutch oven from its hook and place it on the hearth before placing the dough in it, taking care not to burn your hands on the hot pot. Put the lid on, and replace the pot on the hook.

Baking time depends on the heat your fire produces during baking time—average cooking time, about 45 minutes. As there is no thermostatic control on fireplace heat, a chain with a hook can be looped around the bailing handle of the Dutch oven to raise and lower it over the fire by using the various chain links on the hook. A little experimenting will show you the correct height above the flame for the heat you need.

2

HOW FIREPLACES AND WOOD STOVES WORK

Although fireplaces and wood stoves are both designed to keep us warm, there's a lot of basic difference in the way they do it. Most of the warmth we get from an ordinary fireplace is radiant heat like the heat of the sun—heat that literally shines on us directly from the flames, and heat that is reflected from the hot sides and back of the fireplace. Very little heating effect results from convection, that is, the circulation of heated air through the room. Much of the air heated by the fire is drawn into the fireplace and carried up the chimney with the smoke. As a result, tests have shown that the plain old-fashioned fireplace is only about a third as efficient as a good wood stove. But efficiency isn't the only consideration. The cheeriness and charm of an open fire are important, too. Often they're more important to the homeowner than efficiency. And, fortunately, there's a way to have a reasonable degree of both.

MODIFIED FIREPLACES

To retain the atmosphere of the open fire while increasing its efficiency, "modi-fied" fireplaces were developed long ago, though the term is seldom used now. One of these is the "circulating fireplace" developed centuries ago in France, as described in Chapter 1. Although modern versions vary in design, the principle is the same. A metal air chamber is built into the fireplace with its walls exposed to the flames. Room air, heated in this chamber, expands and rises, returning to the room through registers near the top of the fireplace or above it, drawing in replacement air through openings near the bottom. So a steady flow of heated air circulates through the room as long as there's a fire in the fireplace. And, of course, the fire provides radiant heat, as usual. The result is greatly increased heating efficiency. Yet the fireplace looks the same as ever.

Another modified fireplace type is the Franklin stove, also called a Franklin fireplace by some manufacturers. Essentially, this is an iron fireplace set out from the wall of a room and connected to the chimney by a metal flue pipe. Room air heated by the metal body of the unit circulates by natural convection, producing much the same overall heating effect as the circulat-

Fig. 11. A Franklin stove in the true sense of the word. Doors are closed, but draft adjuster openings at bottom of center doors provide considerable control. To see the fire, leave the doors open. Portland Stove Foundry, Inc.

Fig. 12. Call it a Franklin fireplace. This one has a grate, lets you see the flames. Damper is built into the cast iron assembly on top of the unit. Portland Stove Foundry, Inc.

ing fireplace. The appearance of the Franklin stove, of course, differs considerably from that of a modern fireplace. But its design suits it to many decorative themes, and it has the advantage of easy installation. Often, where its added efficiency is the important factor, the opening of an existing masonry fireplace is closed with a metal panel through which the Franklin stove's flue pipe is led to the original fireplace chimney.

WHAT NOT TO EXPECT OF A FIREPLACE

Neither the fireplace (ordinary or circulating) nor the Franklin stove provide much control over the rate at which the fire burns. When they're open at the front to provide a full view of the fire, they admit combustion air freely, so the fire is unimpeded. There's no really effective way of slowing it down to prolong it, except to the degree possible by closing the metal doors of a Franklin stove. But not all of them have doors. The best you can do with a

fireplace is to use a firescreen to slow the draft, or close the damper a notch or two as the fire dies down to bring about a proportionate reduction in the heat loss up the chimney. But you have to do this with care. If you close the damper too much you'll have a smoky room. If there's a bed of ashes under a waning fire, however, it serves to insulate the unburned wood, often sufficiently to provide enough glowing embers to start a new fire the next morning, after the addition of a little kindling.

HOW TO START A FIRE IN A FIREPLACE

There are a number of ways to start a fire in a fireplace. Whichever one you use, you're likely to find it will cause an argument with the first person who sees you do it. The subject is a controversial one, a fact that adds zest to the fire. But don't worry. All you need is a method that works, and most of them do.

Perhaps the commonest method calls for crumpled paper on the hearth between

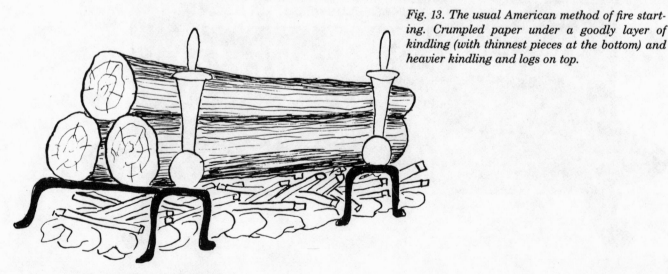

Fig. 13. The usual American method of fire starting. Crumpled paper under a goodly layer of kindling (with thinnest pieces at the bottom) and heavier kindling and logs on top.

the andirons as the starting layer. Kindling is laid on top of the paper, arranged to allow free air circulation when the paper is lighted. This is usually arranged with one layer at right angles to the next, so air space is assured. A double layer, or 1½-2″ of kindling (depending on the thickness of the wood) is ordinarily enough. But don't skimp on the kindling. Too little kindling is one of the commonest causes of no-start fireplace fires. Use plenty of it if you want to be sure.

Place at least three logs on top of the paper and the kindling. These can be small wood logs or manufactured logs, or merely oversized pieces of kindling wood. But don't expect to get a good fire from a single wooden log. It's the funneling of flame through the spaces between logs that gets the whole thing going. As the flame races through the narrow space between the logs it ignites the surface of the logs, after which the fire keeps itself going.

If you want a small but cheery fire for a short period, as before dinner, use small stuff like cut-up lengths of fallen branches—the kind of thing old timers think of as large pieces of kindling. To start

it all you simply light the crumpled paper. You can get a worthwhile fire with a cheery glow this way, and you can have it crackling in a few minutes. It won't last long, but it won't waste wood, and if you only want it for a short period it does the trick. If you decide to extend your fireside session, all you need to do is add some firewood to have the basis for a full evening's fire.

Another method that also works nicely, and is even more likely to be the subject of debate, is a method often used in England and parts of New England. This calls for the usual layer of crumpled newspaper between the andirons or log rests. Two logs are then laid parallel across the log rest, over the crumpled paper. The kindling is laid across the two logs, to make a platform for the third log that runs parallel to the first two and rests between them. To make sure the kindling lights, a fair number of kindling sticks are tilted so as to poke down into the crumpled paper. You light the paper as usual, and if your logs are seasoned, you've got your fire.

Fig. 14. An English variation. Two bottom logs with kindling laid across them, a top log on the kindling and a few pieces of kindling poking down into the crumpled paper below. Light the paper and the fire travels up the kindling and gets the fire under way.

THE WOOD STOVE—HOW TO CONTROL IT FOR CONTINUOUS HEAT

If you want to keep a wood fire going on a steady night-and-day basis, you need the combustion control provided by a true wood stove. This amounts mainly to an adjustable entrance opening for the combustion air, usually called the draft adjuster or draft door. (It's often the door also used for ash removal.) Located at or below the base of the firebox (as is the ash compartment) the door is usually hinged for ash removal and also fitted with a slotted plate that slides or revolves to uncover the draft openings. (A handle or knob operates it.)

When the plate is adjusted to uncover the openings completely, the air flow, or draft, into the base of the fire is at its maximum. This produces a hot, fast-burning fire. As the plate is adjusted to close the draft openings partially or completely, the fire is slowed. This reduces the heat output and also results in greatly extended burning time. This, plus an ample supply of firewood in the stove, makes it possible to "hold" a fire overnight or longer, so that it can be kept going merely by adding more wood and removing the ashes. For additional heat, of course, the draft can be opened farther whenever necessary. But don't expect to hold a hot, fast fire overnight. For extended burning time you need a slow fire. You can't have everything.

In traditional cast-iron stoves, like the familiar potbelly type, the draft door and its adjusting plate, even when closed, allow sufficient air to pass to maintain a slow fire as they are not intended to produce an absolute seal. So individual models have their own "personalities." To get the knack of adjusting them for maximum burning time, therefore, you need a little practice, but it isn't difficult.

"SECONDARY" AIR

The term "secondary" air, while not a part of the old timer's wood-stove terminology, is a technical term now often used to designate the extra air admitted directly over the fire. In many traditional wood stoves, this air is admitted through adjustable openings in the fueling door—the larger door, higher up on the stove than the draft or ash door. As the extra air serves two purposes you'll probably be dealing with it. It provides combustion air to burn the gases and vapors that may be driven out of the wood, unburned by the initial burning process, as described later in regard to "creosote" deposits. It can also be used to slow the fire quickly, when required. Opened to a moderate degree, the secondary air openings admit air for burning off the unburned vapors without an unwanted cooling effect on the fire. Opened wide, they allow a great volume of cool air to enter, slowing both the draft and the fire. This is done only for short periods during which the draft adjustment is kept closed. The procedure comes in handy when it's necessary to slow a hot fire as quickly as possible. Once the fire is at a moderate level, the openings are adjusted for efficient burning. If the stove doesn't have a secondary air adjustment, you can open the fueling door a little to get the same fire-retarding effect. But keep an eye open for sparks that may pop out.

(Some wood burning heaters of more recent design, often called "airtight" heaters, provide for tighter closure of their control openings, for thermostatic operation.)

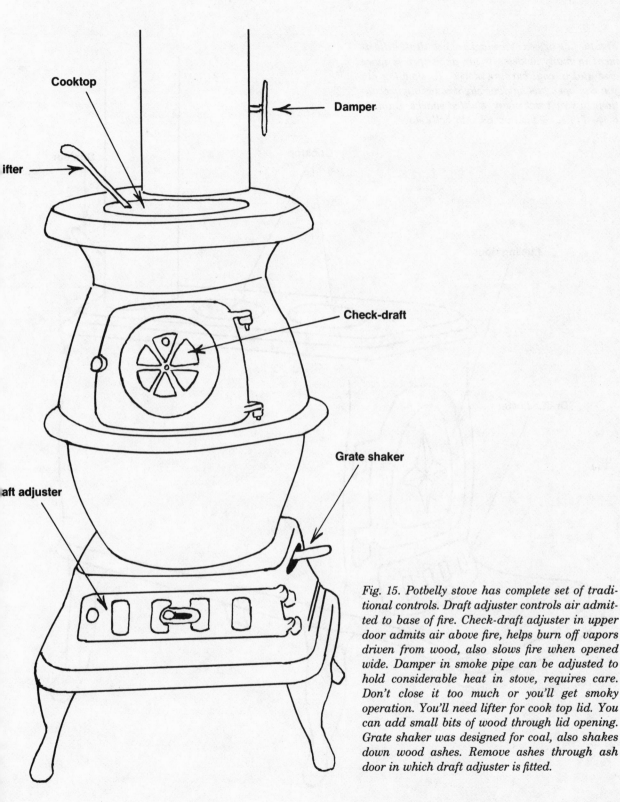

Cooktop

Damper

ifter

Check-draft

Grate shaker

aft adjuster

Fig. 15. Potbelly stove has complete set of traditional controls. Draft adjuster controls air admitted to base of fire. Check-draft adjuster in upper door admits air above fire, helps burn off vapors driven from wood, also slows fire when opened wide. Damper in smoke pipe can be adjusted to hold considerable heat in stove, requires care. Don't close it too much or you'll get smoky operation. You'll need lifter for cook top lid. You can add small bits of wood through lid opening. Grate shaker was designed for coal, also shakes down wood ashes. Remove ashes through ash door in which draft adjuster is fitted.

Fig. 16. Log or box stove lacks check-draft adjustment in many models, as air above fire is more essential in coal burning stoves. To slow log fire you can open fueling door slightly, taking precautions to keep track of any emitted sparks. Damper is used in same manner as with belly stove.

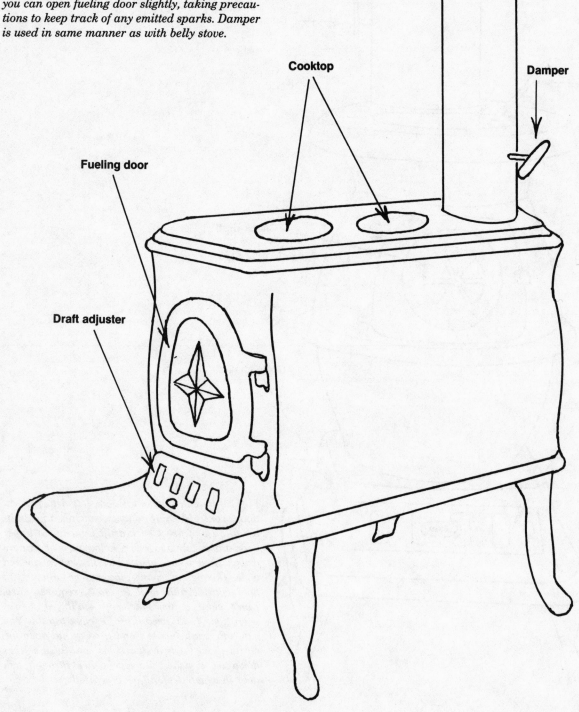

Cooktop

Damper

Fueling door

Draft adjuster

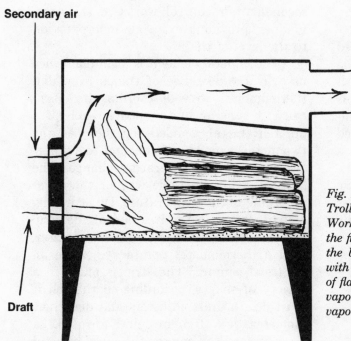

Secondary air

Draft

Fig. 17. Wood stoves like the imported Jotul and Trolla, and domestic models from Wilton Stove Works and others, have a metal partition above the fire area, so logs burn from the front toward the back, like cigarettes, for a long-lasting fire with moderate heat output. Extra travel distance of flame and flue gases burn off creosote-causing vapors. Secondary air inlet provides oxygen for vapor burning.

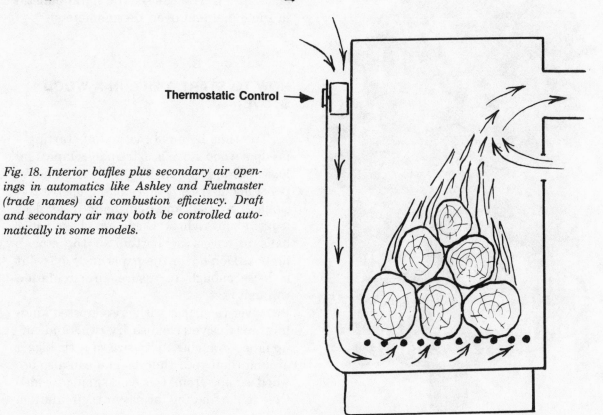

Thermostatic Control →

Fig. 18. Interior baffles plus secondary air openings in automatics like Ashley and Fuelmaster (trade names) aid combustion efficiency. Draft and secondary air may both be controlled automatically in some models.

How Fireplaces and Wood Stoves Work   29

AUTOMATIC WOOD STOVES

Some wood stoves (now also called wood burning heaters) are available equipped with automatic controls for both draft and secondary air. As the controls operate directly from heat-responsive "bimetal" elements, no electricity is required by the automatic control. You simply set a control dial to the heat level you want. When the fire in the stove heats up above the level you have set, the draft adjuster automatically closes, slowing the fire. The

Fig. 19. Ashley automatic wood heater. The louvered box protruding from door contains the thermostatic control. The same company makes a variety of automatics, including modern styles.

secondary air control works in the same manner, providing extra air in proportion to the level of the fire.

(The bimetal element is a simple device used in a wide range of things from dial thermometers to wall thermostats. Basically, it consists of two strips, each of a different metal, bonded together. As the two metals expand and contract to a different extent with temperature changes, the bimetal strip bends one way or the other according to the temperature. By attaching a shaft or rod to the free end of the strip you can harness it to open a draft adjuster, turn a thermometer pointer, or make an electrical contact. The strip is made in a variety of shapes, according to the job it must do. In draft adjusters and dial thermometers it's often in spiral form like a clock spring. You can see the spiral bimetal in some dial and oven thermometers.)

HOW TO START A FIRE IN A WOOD STOVE

The time honored method of starting a fire in a wood stove is extremely simple and logical. Start by bunching up balls of newspaper about the size of a small grapefruit. A single sheet (left and right hand page) does it just about right. Use enough of the paper balls to cover the bottom of the stove's firebox. Don't jam the paper in. You want it loose enough to assure air circulation through it.

Cover the paper with criss-crossed kindling. For this you can use dry twigs and cut-up fallen branches up to sizes a little bigger around than your thumb. You can also use wood scraps from the workshop provided they're not too big for easy air circulation.

Short lengths up to the size of what's called 1 x 2 are good on top of the thinner pieces. Soft woods like pine and cedar make especially good kindling because they light easily and burn fast. In most stoves a layer of kindling about an inch-and-a-half deep on top of the paper is usually enough if the full-size firewood is dry. As to the firewood, use smaller pieces directly on top of the kindling, with a few larger pieces on top of them. Again, don't jam the stove. You can add more wood after the fire gets going.

Be *sure* the damper in the flue pipe or in the stove is open *all the way* and that the draft openings in the draft door are also open all the way. Then open the draft door and light the paper in several places, shut the draft door, leaving the draft openings open, and leave it alone. If you yield to the temptation to keep opening the fueling door to see how the fire's doing, you may chill it so much you'll put it out.

Important: If the weather is very cold or if the stove hasn't been used for a time, you may find that cold air is actually moving *down* the chimney. One way to find out is by lighting a match and holding it inside the firebox through the fueling door *before* you build the fire. If a downdraft points the flame down or blows it out, a preliminary step is called for. This step consists of placing one or two balls of paper, sized as described earlier, in the bottom of the firebox and lighting them. Be sure the flue pipe damper and draft adjuster are open, and close the fueling door after you light the paper balls. This procedure gradually starts some warm air moving up the chimney. Don't use a large amount of paper, as it may send smoke into the room through crevices in the stove before the chimney draft gets going. Once you feel a little heat in the metal flue pipe (don't burn your

fingers) you can burn a couple more paper balls. Be sure no glowing sparks remain when you start to build your fire, or it may get going before you want it to. As a final step with a cold chimney, you can light one more paper ball *on top* of the *heavy* firewood before you light the paper *under* the kindling. This won't light the firewood, but it will usually re-establish the chimney draft. Then when you light the paper under the kindling you'll avoid smoking up the room. If possible, take a peek at the burning paper on top of the heavy firewood to be sure the fire and smoke are headed up the flue pipe. (How well you can peek depends on the stove design.)

CAUTION: Don't pour flammable liquids on your paper, kindling or firewood, even on the advice of some stove wizard. The liquid can not only flare up and cause trouble, it may also vaporize, then suddenly ignite and blow up the stove. Liquid starters are for open charcoal braziers out of doors, *not* for wood stoves.

After your fire is established adjust your draft openings for the heat level you want. A wood stove can produce more heat than you may realize, even to the extent of glowing cherry red around the firebox—which can create problems. So watch your draft adjustment carefully while you become familiar with stove operation. As a newcomer to wood stove use you're more likely to face the problems of overheating than underheating. If the room gets too hot for comfort in the early stages, open a window, or a door that allows the excess heat to flow into another area of the house.

ONE FINAL CAUTION: if your kindling burns to smoldering embers without starting your logs, but continues to emit a sizeable volume of smoke from the chimney, *do not* open the fueling door to see what's going on inside the stove. The smoke may contain highly flammable vapor driven out of the logs by the heat of the glowing embers. Because of an inadequate air supply (due to the sluggish draft produced by the smoldering fire), this vapor often drifts unburned up the chimney with the smoke. Under these conditions, if you open the fueling door, the inrush of air may cause the vapor to ignite with almost explosive suddenness, spewing a sheet of flame into the room (and possibly into your face), sometimes also blowing glowing particles out through the draft door openings. All this is most likely to happen with green or pitchy logs, but don't take a chance anyway. Let the fire go out. With this kind of poor start it usually doesn't last long. Then start a new one with plenty of paper and kindling and seasoned, non-pitchy logs.

ABOUT GRATES

Since you may not always be able to buy the specific wood stove you'd like, you may wind up with a stove intended for coal. The usual potbelly stove is an example. In this event you'll find a coal grate in the base of the firebox. But don't worry about it. Wood burns beautifully on top of a coal grate if you remember to take the ashes out before they pile up high enough in the ash compartment to reach the grate. When they get that high they prevent the incoming air from cooling the grate, and the heat of the fire can burn it out. So take your ashes out often enough to prevent it. There's an advantage to the grate, too, in that you can burn coal if you want to—and if you can get it.

The usual stove designed for wood, such as the common box stove (sometimes called a log stove), doesn't have a grate. You usually build the fire on the metal bottom of the stove or on an inner bottom that may be in the form of a metal platform with holes in it. If any instructions come with the stove you buy, follow them. Some suggest covering the bottom of the firebox with about an inch of sand or gravel before you start your fire. This insulates the bottom to some extent and reduces the amount of heat that reaches the floor under the stove. Also, it keeps the fire out of direct contact with the metal bottom of the firebox. The old time log-burning stoves, however, (and their contemporary counterparts) can usually withstand the heat without ill effects. Many have been doing it for a generation or more. Details on safety clearances of nearby flammable surfaces are covered in Chapter 5.

II
How to Build and Install Fireplaces

3

HOW TO BUILD A MASONRY FIREPLACE AND CHIMNEY

Many successful masonry fireplaces have been built by homeowners, with and without professional assistance. The all-important preliminary, however, is establishing the correct proportions for the fireplace and the correct flue size to go with it. The fireplace diagram and the dimension chart keyed to it (see figs. 20 and 21) give you the correct proportions and flue sizes for a wide range of fireplace sizes. As to the size you choose, pick one that's suited to the proportions of the room. If you're in doubt, measure an existing fireplace, as in a neighbor's home, that seems right in a similar room. The usual mistake is in building "a great big fireplace" in a relatively small room. If you build a full-sized fire in it, you'll probably find it makes the room too hot. If you build an undersized fire in it, most of the heat goes up the chimney. And, of course, big fireplaces call for bigger and costlier flues and use up expensive big logs. The fireplaces in the photos in this chapter provide an idea of size for average rooms. If you build a fireplace with a front opening a yard wide and 32″ high, one of the sizes listed in the chart, you can burn logs in the readily available 16-20″ length range. And if you want to create the effect of a larger fireplace, you can do it by making the facings of the fireplace wider.

FOOTINGS

Before you start your fireplace job check your local building code for chimney footing requirements. In case there's no code in your area, make your footing of poured concrete 6″ larger than the outside dimensions of the fireplace all around, 12″ thick, and level. If the footing is outside of the house it must be at a depth below that to which the ground freezes (called the frost line).

THE FOUNDATION

After the footing has hardened, the foundation of the fireplace is built up from the footing. Insofar as possible, plan the

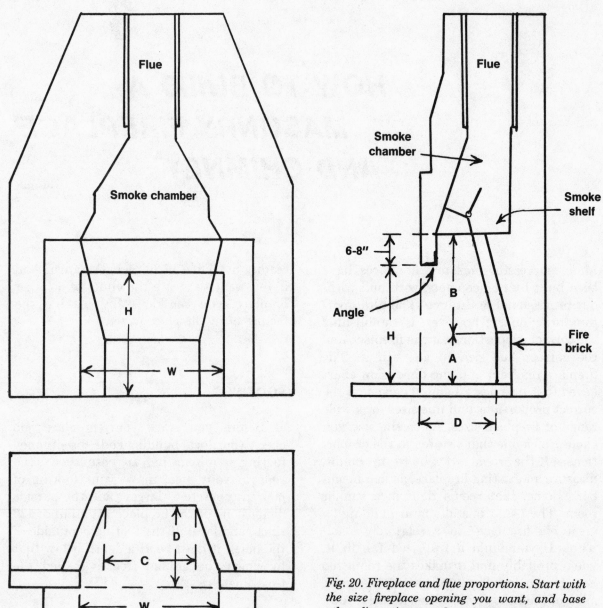

Fig. 20. Fireplace and flue proportions. Start with the size fireplace opening you want, and base other dimensions on that. Angles will then take care of themselves. There's some leeway in the figures, so don't be surprised if you find some variation between this and other guides. But be wary of wide variations.

Fig. 21. Apply the figures in this chart to the lettered fireplace parts in the drawings. Don't skimp on flue size.

Width W	Height H	Depth D	Minimum back (horizontal) C	Vertical back wall A	Inclined back wall B	Outside dimensions of standard rectangular flue lining	Inside diameter of standard round flue lining
INCHES	INCHES	INCHES	INCHES	INCHES	INCHES	INCHES	INCHES
24	24	16-18	14	14	16	8½ x 8½	10
28	24	16-18	14	14	16	8½ x 8½	10
24	28	16-18	14	14	20	8½ x 8½	10
30	28	16-18	16	14	20	8½ x 13	10
36	28	16-18	22	14	20	8½ x 13	12
42	28	16-18	28	14	20	8½ x 18	12
36	32	18-20	20	14	24	8½ x 18	12
42	32	18-20	26	14	24	13 x 13	12
48	32	18-20	32	14	24	13 x 13	15
42	36	18-20	26	14	28	13 x 13	15
48	36	18-20	32	14	28	13 x 18	15
54	36	18-20	38	14	28	13 x 18	15
60	36	18-20	44	14	28	13 x 18	15
42	40	20-22	24	17	29	13 x 13	15
48	40	20-22	30	17	29	13 x 18	15
54	40	20-22	36	17	29	13 x 18	15
60	40	20-22	42	17	29	18 x 18	18
66	40	20-22	48	17	29	18 x 18	18
72	40	22-28	51	17	29	18 x 18	18

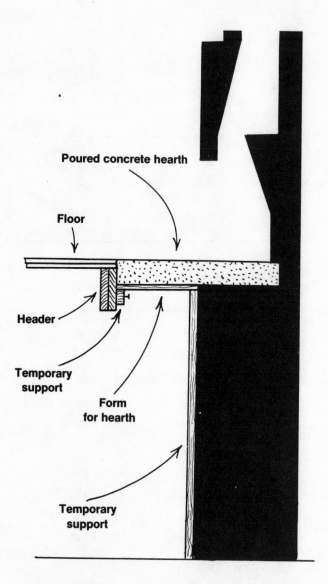

Poured concrete hearth

Floor

Header

Temporary support

Form for hearth

Temporary support

Fig. 22. Fireplace, hearth and chimney are supported entirely by fireplace foundation. Cantilevered concrete hearth may be supported temporarily (while hardening) by wood and plywood, as shown. All combustible supports must be removed for fire safety after concrete hardens. Concrete should be reinforced with metal rods as shown in Fig. 49.

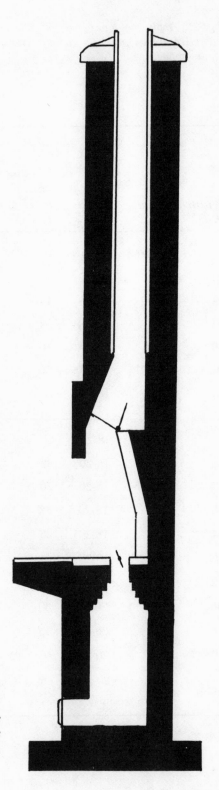

Fig. 23. Fireplace and chimney is built like a stone tower, complete in itself, not supported by the house framing. It must be able to stand independently, regardless of settling of house.

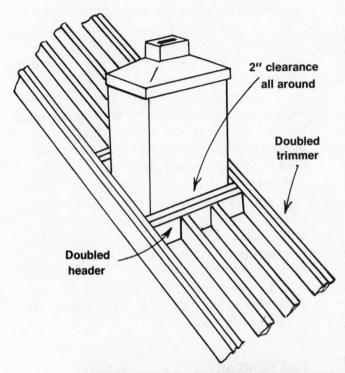

2" clearance all around

Doubled trimmer

Doubled header

Fig. 24. Wherever chimney passes through floor or roof rafters or joists, headers between them are doubled, as trimmers must support load on intervening members. Clearance of 2" between masonry and wood is required. This is intended to prevent heat transfer from chimney (or fireplace) to wood framing, also to provide for uneven settling of house and chimney foundation.

Fig. 25. Start of fireplace in new home. Basement wall has been jogged out over fireplace footing to provide space for ashpit. If fireplace was to be added to existing house, ashpit and foundation would be built on outside of house foundation over suitable footing.

foundation so the masonry blocks can be laid with a minimum of block-cutting. If you're doing the job yourself, you'll usually find masonry block the easiest material to use. Where foundation is built up from a basement footing, it also serves as the ash pit, so you build it with an opening at the base of the front wall (corresponding to the front of the fireplace) for a readymade metal ash door. You won't need to empty the ash pit often, as wood ashes accumulate very slowly. But buy an ash door big enough for a standard shovel, and use the door to plan the size of the opening into which it will be cemented as the foundation progresses. (The instructions that follow are based on a foundation for a fireplace only. If a central heating flue must also be accommodated in the foundation and chimney (see fig. 35), it must be planned from the beginning, as flue tiles must be set in place as described later, during the construction of the foundation.)

If there's only a "crawl space" under the first floor of the house, instead of a basement, the foundation from the footing will, of course, not be as high, nor will it be accessible from inside. It can still serve as a small ash pit, however, with the ash door installed on the foundation wall outside of the house, assuming the fireplace is built into an outside wall.

HOW TO LAY MASONRY BLOCK

To start, lay out the first course of block "dry," on the footing. Use a taut string to align them for straightness, and use a large square (like a framing square available from hardware stores) to square the corners in the position they will occupy when cemented. Then make a heavy pencil mark on the footing along the base of the blocks.

The most widely used block size is normally 8 x 8 x 16". The blocks are actually ⅜" shorter than this, however, to allow for a mortar joint ⅜" thick. To get the blocks spaced properly (allowing for the mortar end joints), lay the first course of blocks on top of the footing "dry," and move them as needed to get the spaces even. Again, use a taut string, tied from the corner blocks to get them in a straight line. And use the square to get the corners square. Then pencil-mark the foundation at the base of each block at each end to help you replace them in the same position when you start cementing. Extend the corner marks far enough to show clearly, after the mortar for the first course is spread on the footing.

THE MORTAR

A typical mortar mix for block work consists of two parts masonry cement (this is partly portland cement and partly hydrated lime) to from four to six parts mason's sand. The less sand, the stronger. The purpose of the lime is to add sticking power. If you want extra strength mortar use only about three parts sand. Use just enough water to make the mix apply easily and stick well. A little advance experimenting is the best bet for this. You'll get the knack of mixing the mortar very quickly as you go along.

USING THE MORTAR

To start the actual block laying, spread mortar on the footing along the line where the blocks were tried dry. You can do this a block at a time or several blocks at a time.

Apply the mortar to the footing over the full block width, using a fairly large mason's trowel (the pointed type). To make sure there's ample mortar along the outer edges of the blocks, make a furrow down the center of the mortar layer so as to push more mortar toward the sides. Then trowel mortar on to the end of each block as it is laid to stick it to the one it will join. As you lay each block in the bed of mortar on the footing, use a carpenter's (or mason's) level to make sure the block is level. If it isn't, work the high end down into the mortar until it is. Sometimes you may have to lift the block and place some small stones or block chips under an end, and spread fresh mortar to get it level. The object is to get a full and firm bond between the footing and the first course of block. And the blocks must be level. If you're a beginner, you may have to push some mortar into joints here and there, where gaps show. Use the trowel for this if you can get the job done. If you have to, use your fingers—if you're a newcomer to mason work. The first course of block must be not only level but smooth and even along the tops.

When the first course is complete, spread mortar along the upper side and end edges of the blocks, and on the vertical end edges of the blocks in the next course. Then set each block in place on top of the first course. The blocks are staggered so end joints in the second course are placed above the center of the blocks in the first course. Level each block, as before, and use the taut string to keep a check on the straightness of the walls. Set the cleanout door in place of a block directly above the base of the ash pit. (See fig. 26.) You can buy a tool called a joiner to smooth the mortar into the joints after the blocks are cemented and to make the mortar lines slightly con-

cave. This makes sure the mortar is in good contact with meeting edges, and also gives you a neat job. If you don't want to buy the tool (or you can't find one matched to the ⅜″ mortar thickness), you can make one by simply bending a short piece of nominal ⅜″ soft copper tubing.

As your foundation approaches the level of the floor where the fireplace is to be, you can use solid blocks to cap the walls and to prepare for a concrete hearth that will be finished off even with the floor. As shown in the illustration, the hearth is "cantilevered" from the wall. It can't be supported by the floor, as the floor and the fireplace are supported by different parts of the overall house foundation. If one happens to settle at a different rate from the other, a floor-supported hearth might crack free of

Fig. 26. Job begins with building of wall with masonry blocks to enclose ashpit. Cleanout door at left of wall is for oil burner flue that will be included in chimney. Ash dump door for fireplace is in base of fireplace, as shown in Fig. 36.

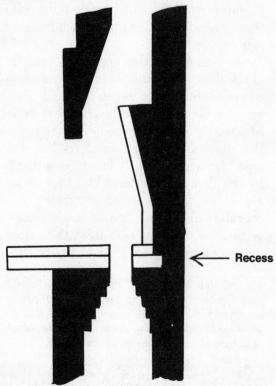

Fig. 27. When poured concrete hearth slab is cantilevered straight out without arch or angle support, leave a hearth-thickness recess across back of fireplace masonry for rear edge of hearth, as shown.

← **Recess**

the fireplace foundation. In older homes the cantilevered portion of the hearth extending forward from the foundation was sometimes supported by a masonry arch built on to the front of the foundation. Today, it is usually a concrete slab poured in a temporary plywood form at hearth level. Iron reinforcing rods embedded in the slab provide extra strength and resistance to cracking. Some are also poured over readymade metal forms that remain in place and serve as additional reinforcement. The hearth should project at least 16″ from the chimney breast and at least 8″ on each side of the fireplace opening. If the fireplace is built on a slab that also serves

as the floor of the house, of course, the hearth is also supported by the slab, and cantilevering isn't necessary. A footing of the full thickness mentioned earlier, however, should be provided under the base of the fireplace-chimney area.

THE FIREPLACE

Two general methods are used in building fireplaces. In one, all mason work is carried out at the same time, so the inside and the outside are completed simultaneously. In the other, the fireplace is "roughed in," then finished inside to its final form. So long as the results are correct, the method is up to the builder. The photos show the inside and outside masonry progressing together. The drawings show the steps in roughing the fireplace, then finishing the inside to final form. Whichever method you follow, be sure that the inside proportions and angles are maintained as indicated in the fireplace diagram and chart (see figs. 20 and 21).

The hearth, back, and sides of the fireplace are lined with fire brick (different from ordinary brick) and cemented with fire clay. (You can buy the fire clay at the masonry supplier where you buy the fire bricks.)

If there is an ash pit inside the foundation under the fireplace, a ready-made, hinged "ash dump" is mounted in the hearth. This is roughly the size of one fire brick, and usually takes the place of one. In pouring the concrete hearth, however, you must provide an opening for it. This can be done easily with a scrap wood form. Buy the ash dump before the hearth is poured, so you can be sure of the opening size required.

Fig. 28. Looking down from floor above, you see top of ashpit-enclosing wall of masonry block, also first section of flue lining for oil burner flue. Flue lining for oil burner must start at least 8" below point where horizontal section of oil burner flue enters chimney. You can see the backyard through opening where fireplace will be built.

Fig. 29. Chimney flue liners stored at masonry supplier's storage yard. Buy the size your fireplace requires, as many as chimney height requires.

Fig. 30. Oil burner is connected to square vertical flue liner with round section of horizontal tile, as shown. Oil burner flue will run upward through rear left corner of fireplace masonry. Hole has been cut in vertical flue to take round flue tile.

Fig. 31. Connector thimbles for flues of heating units. These are just long enough to run through masonry block in chimneys where vertical flue is directly behind block. Where flue is farther back, as in top photo, longer section of liner is used.

Fig. 32. From above. Masonry blocks to right of flue will support hearth slab. Space between them will be ashpit.

Fig. 33. Concrete hearth slab has been poured on metal form to cap ashpit and extend to front of floor opening, Mason is troweling surface smooth slightly below floor level to take masonry to follow. Note form that provides ash dump opening through slab.

Fig. 34. As fireplace will have raised hearth, course of masonry block is laid over slab, solid blocks over fireplace area. Mason is spreading mortar for blocks that will abut oil burner flue liner. Boards have been laid over hearth front to bring working surface even with flooring. Ash dump opening is left between blocks.

Fig. 35. Next section of oil burner flue liner is now set in place. Liners for all flues must be set in place ahead of surrounding masonry so ends of liner sections can be sealed together with mortar.

Fig. 36. With oil burner flue liner section in place, firebricks are being laid on fire clay on floor of fireplace area. Ready-made metal ash dump with hinge-pivot door has been set in opening, to be cemented. Outside brickwork of fireplace is being built up as inside progresses.

Fig. 37. First course of firebrick sides and back now goes in place over firebrick floor, all cemented with fire clay.

Fig. 38. As sides and back are built up, outer wall keeps pace. Note level on outer wall. All brick-work is checked course by course, with level. One used for firebrick rests against wall at right. Masonry will be built out at sides to wood spacer strips which can be removed after cement hardens, to provide clearance between masonry and framing, where required by code.

Fig. 39. Rear fireplace wall has now taken forward slope, starting from top of vertical portion about 14" above bricked fireplace floor. Start of forward slope varies with fireplace size, as shown in chart on page 37.

Fig. 40. Firebrick interior of fireplace has been completed. Note slope of top course of brick at fireplace back. Note also that half bricks are used to make brickwork come even at front and corners. Bricks are cut in half with a wide chisel called a brick set. Use a hammer to drive it into brick corners, then to make cuts across the surfaces. A sharp whack then breaks the brick at the cut line. Practice on a few bricks first.

THE DAMPER

As shown in the drawings and the fireplace diagram (see figs. 20 and 21), the back of the fireplace slopes forward, usually from a point a little more than a foot above the hearth. (Below that the back is vertical.) The slope reflects the fire heat downward into the room, brings the damper position (and flue entrance) forward, and also provides the smoke shelf shown in previous chapters. Buy your damper when you decide on the fireplace size, and have it on hand as the job progresses. As shown in the photos, clearance (filled with fiberglass) is allowed at the damper ends to permit expansion and contraction with changes in temperature. Do not use the damper to support the masonry of the fireplace front

above the opening. This would place the damper practically even with the top of the fireplace opening, and allow smoke to escape into the room. As shown in the drawing, the fireplace front masonry above the opening should be supported by a heavy length of 3 x 3 x 3/16" angle iron with its ends resting on the vertical masonry at each side of the opening. (For fireplace openings of 4' width or more, use 3½ x 3½ x 5/16".) The damper should be set about 4 to 8" above the top of the fireplace opening to minimize the chance of smoky operation, especially in windy weather. The back flange of the damper should be supported entirely by the masonry of the smoke shelf to protect it from the intense heat of the fire. The

Fig. 41. The ready-made damper is now set in place on top of the bricks. Use cement to keep it in place, but allow clearance at the ends for expansion of the cast iron. Fill in the space between damper ends and the cement with fiberglass. This seals it without blocking expansion, causing cracks.

Fig. 42. Brickwork on outside is built up to match interior masonry. Typical codes permit chimney to be built in contact with house wall sheathing if masonry is thick enough, commonly 8″ or more.

How to Build a Masonry Fireplace and Chimney   51

tapered hollow portion from the damper up to the point where the flue tiles begin is called the smoke chamber. Although older fireplaces were often built with only the single metal angle iron section supporting the fireplace breast and the masonry above it, you'll be wise to install a second angle across the front of the masonry at about mantel height. This adds reinforcement and provides extra support for the weight of the chimney above it. (Experienced masons can judge whether the extra angle is needed, depending on the width and form of the fireplace and smoke chamber, but in do-it-yourself work it's best to play safe.) The cross section drawing of the fireplace and smoke chamber show the angle positions in a typical fireplace. Note, too, that a recess is left for the rear of the hearth slab, if the slab extension in front of the fireplace is flat, without a supporting arch under the extended portion.

Fig. 43. Fireplace front is now bricked. A 3" x 3" length of angle iron resting on the brickwork at the fireplace sides supports the brickwork above the fireplace opening, as shown earlier in drawing. This support is 4"-8" below the damper to prevent fireplace from smoking. Do not use damper to support brickwork. Metal masonry ties are laid in the mortar between bricks at intervals. These protrude from brickwork to take the final decorative brick facing that goes over this. After cement hardens at this stage wood spacer pieces can be removed to provide clearance where required by code.

Fig. 44. Final face brick has been carried all the way to ceiling, bonded to bricks behind it with mortar and masonry ties. Wood supports for mantel project through brick from header behind it. Length of scrap lumber resting on the supports shows height of mantel to come. Raised hearth has been built up on poured concrete supporting slab.

Fig. 46. Completed chimney. Note that scaffolding can be built up to required height. If you plan your own chimney job, you can rent scaffolding. (Figs. 25, 26, 28-46 courtesy of Richard Jowdy, Danbury Gallery of Homes.)

ANOTHER METHOD: ROUGHING IN FIRST

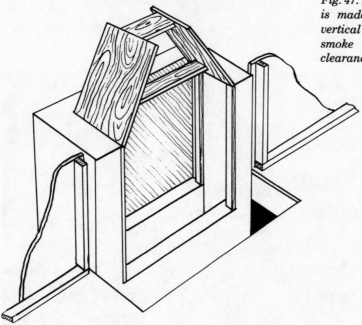

Fig. 47. If fireplace is roughed in before inner form is made, it starts like this. Wood form atop vertical side walls provides support for sides of smoke chamber while cement hardens. Note clearance between wood framing and masonry.

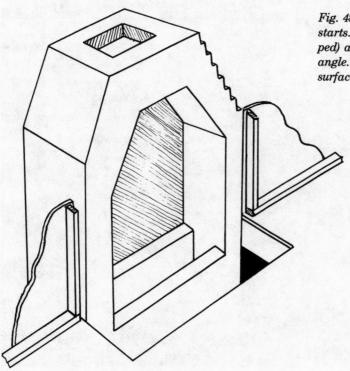

Fig. 48. Rough masonry is built up to where flue starts. If of brick, it is corbelled (bricks overlapped) as shown on right side, to produce required angle. Cement laid on wood form smoothes inner surface of corbelled brickwork.

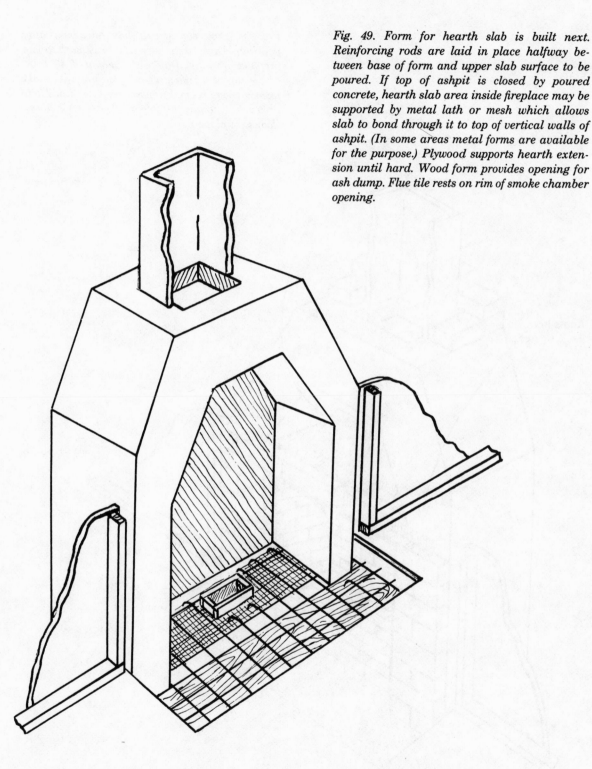

Fig. 49. Form for hearth slab is built next. Reinforcing rods are laid in place halfway between base of form and upper slab surface to be poured. If top of ashpit is closed by poured concrete, hearth slab area inside fireplace may be supported by metal lath or mesh which allows slab to bond through it to top of vertical walls of ashpit. (In some areas metal forms are available for the purpose.) Plywood supports hearth extension until hard. Wood form provides opening for ash dump. Flue tile rests on rim of smoke chamber opening.

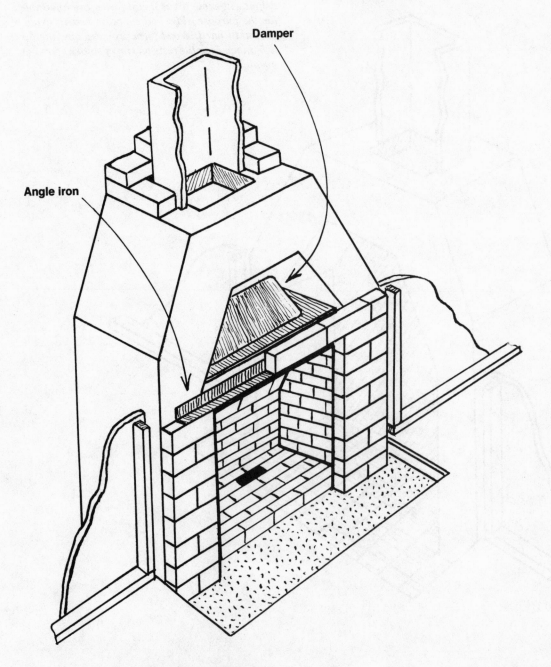

Fig. 50. *Concrete hearth has hardened after pouring. Angle iron supports brickwork above fireplace opening. Damper is mounted 4″ to 8″ above top of fireplace opening to prevent smoke from entering room. Fireplace has been lined with firebrick. Chimney brickwork begins. Ash dump door is in place.*

Damper

Angle iron

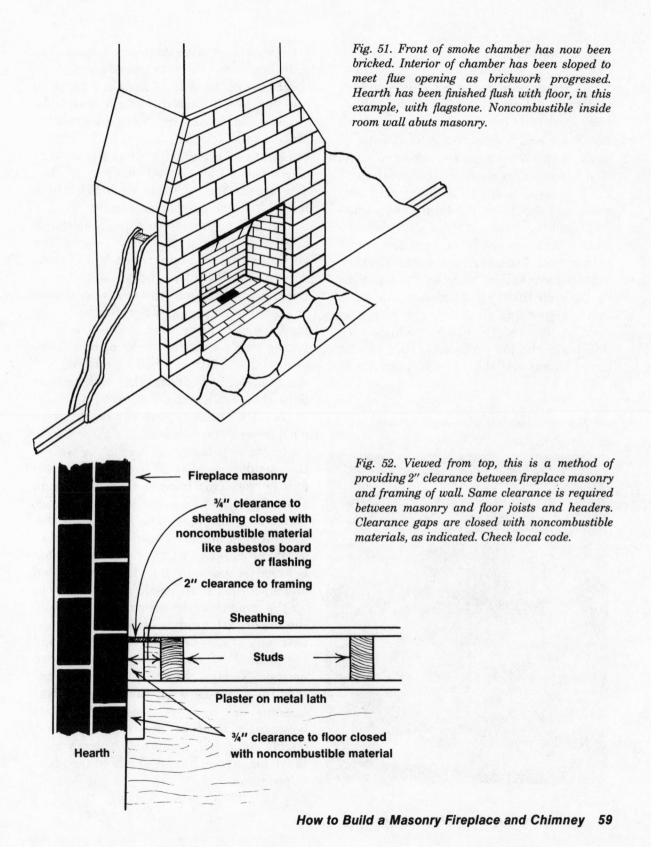

Fig. 51. Front of smoke chamber has now been bricked. Interior of chamber has been sloped to meet flue opening as brickwork progressed. Hearth has been finished flush with floor, in this example, with flagstone. Noncombustible inside room wall abuts masonry.

Fireplace masonry

¾″ clearance to sheathing closed with noncombustible material like asbestos board or flashing

2″ clearance to framing

Sheathing

Studs

Plaster on metal lath

¾″ clearance to floor closed with noncombustible material

Hearth

Fig. 52. Viewed from top, this is a method of providing 2″ clearance between fireplace masonry and framing of wall. Same clearance is required between masonry and floor joists and headers. Clearance gaps are closed with noncombustible materials, as indicated. Check local code.

THE CHIMNEY

As regulations regarding chimney construction details vary somewhat, check your local code in advance. In general, all woodwork and framing must be at least 2″ away from the chimney masonry. The chimney masonry shouldn't be less than 8″ thick, measuring from the flue lining outward, and should be of solid masonry units (not hollow ones). If you use chimney blocks that are made as complete units with a central opening for the flue tile, they usually have hollow areas, as shown in fig. 65, to keep their weight in a manageable range. Depending on your local code, you may be required to fill the hollows with cement as the job progresses. Half blocks, however, are available in solid form. These

Fig. 53. Two-piece solid chimney blocks weigh less per half-unit. They are also made in most flue sizes.

are laid in pairs, with their vertical seams at right angles in alternate courses.

If your chimney is to contain more than one flue, you'll have to build it with individual solid blocks or bricks in order to make it the required size. The blocks or bricks must be laid with what the masons often call "shove-ahead mortar joints." This means that you lay each brick in a full-width bed of mortar (on the course below) and push it down firmly enough to squeeze a little mortar out beyond the vertical surface. (You smooth it off later.) After each brick is laid, mortar is applied to the end that will join the next one. (Some workers prefer to apply the mortar to the joining end of each brick before it is laid.) Either way, successive bricks or blocks are pushed down into the bed of mortar, and simultaneously against the end mortar joint that bonds it to the preceding brick. With a little practice, you can do this with a single wrist movement.

If you're using brick it must be wetted thoroughly and allowed to surface-dry before laying. This prevents the brick from absorbing the water out of the mortar, weakening the joint. The sections of flue lining are set in place ahead of the masonry as it progresses, with end-to-end joints between sections of flue lining cemented and smoothed from inside. It's possible to do the smoothing by reaching down from the top of each newly added section. In the past, any spaces between the flue tile and the brickwork were filled in solid with mortar. Today, the NFPA recommends that the space between the liners and the masonry not be filled, but that the joints between sections of flue liners be thoroughly cemented, using only enough mortar to make a good joint and hold the liners in position.

If two adjoining flues in the same chimney are separated only by the flue liners (without bricking between them), the joints between sections must be staggered by at least 7″ so that no joints coincide. If there are more than two flues in the same chimney, masonry wythes (partitions) at least 4″ thick must be built into the chimney so that there are no more than two flues without wythes between them. If, for example, you have three flues, two of them can be separated simply by the flue liners with staggered joints, but the third one must be separated from the other two by a partitioning wythe.

The top of the chimney must be at least 3′ above the high side of the roof (if it passes through it) or 3′ above the high side of the roof if it is built against a gable end. The chimney top must also be at least 2′ higher than any portion of the building or roof within 10′ of it.

Fig. 54. Solid rectangular masonry blocks for building larger chimneys.

SMOKE TEST

After the chimney is completed it should be given a smoke test to determine whether there are any leaks through the masonry. (As leaks may be very difficult to remedy, take every precaution to avoid them during the construction work.) To make the test, build a paper, straw, or tar-paper fire in the fireplace, and have a helper on hand to watch the chimney from top to bottom. When the smoke emerges from the chimney, close the top of the flue with a wet blanket. If there are any leaks in the masonry the smoke will then show their location. If there are several flues, only one will be connected to the fire place. Block the top of that one alone to see if there is leakage between it and the other flues. If smoke rises from the others (which do not connect to the fireplace) you will know there's leakage between them. Needless to say, it's much easier to do the masonry work carefully in order to avoid such troubles, as it's much more difficult to correct them than to do the job right in the first place. Ample cement hardening time should be allowed before the smoke test, and the fire used for the test should be planned to provide abundant smoke without excess heat. Too hot a fire without adequate masonry curing time can damage the chimney. You want the smokiest fire you can arrange with as little heat as possible.

ABOUT FRAMING AROUND THE FIREPLACE

Your local code will usually specify the procedure to follow in regard to wood framing around a masonry fireplace. If you don't find the details in the code, ask your building inspector for them, as he (or an assistant) will usually examine the work before it's approved. There is, however, a wide variation in codes (even nationally used ones) and in their interpretation by building departments. Some require as much as a 4″ clearance between the fireplace masonry and its surrounding framing. Others call for a 2″ clearance. And in some areas the masonry may be built in contact with the framing if the masonry is thick enough and of the proper material.

One widely followed approach (if there's no code in your area) requires the 2″ clearance between all wood framing and the masonry. This includes the floor framing around the base of the fireplace, the studs in the wall adjacent to the fireplace sides and the header above the fireplace. It also applies to framing around the chimney if it passes through the ceiling.

The subfloor and the sheathing on the outside of the house wall are usually kept ¾″ from the fireplace masonry if the fireplace protrudes through the outside wall. The gap is then closed with metal flashing. The gap between the masonry and the subfloor is firestopped, as detailed shortly. Noncombustible wallboard or plaster can be brought directly to the masonry inside the house, closing the gap between it and the framing. If the fireplace and chimney are completely inside the house, plaster may be applied directly to the exposed masonry. If the back of the fireplace is within a framed wall, the commonly required gap between framing and masonry is 4″. At floor and ceiling levels all gaps between framing and masonry must be firestopped with noncombustible material. (Firestopping is the closing of gaps that

would permit a house fire to travel upward through the house structure from one level to another.) The firestopping material long recommended by many builders is a 1″ thickness of plaster or mortar on strips of metal lath or wire fabric laid across the space between floor headers and the chimney wall. Figure 52 shows the details. Plaster may be applied directly to the chimney surfaces, however.

You may find, too, that the individual layouts of your fireplace and chimney flues affect the requirements. Where a flue from below passes up through the fireplace ma-

Fig. 55. One-piece solid chimney blocks are made to fit most flue sizes.

Fig. 56. If chimney must take an angled course, bricks or blocks are "corbelled" like this. Center of upper vertical portion of flue must not be farther out than center of outer chimney wall below it. Here, flue is safely within limit. Black areas next to flue liner are filled with cement.

Fig. 57. How flashing is applied to chimney. Cap flashing, separate from base flashing, is inserted in fresh mortar joints, as shown, and bent down over base flashing, with about 4″ overlap. Base flashing is bent outward at least 4″ under roof shingles. All flashing sections overlap in shingle fashion to divert water away from chimney and onto roofing. Dotted lines show overlap of flashing, shingles, etc.

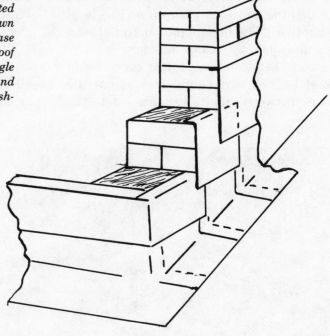

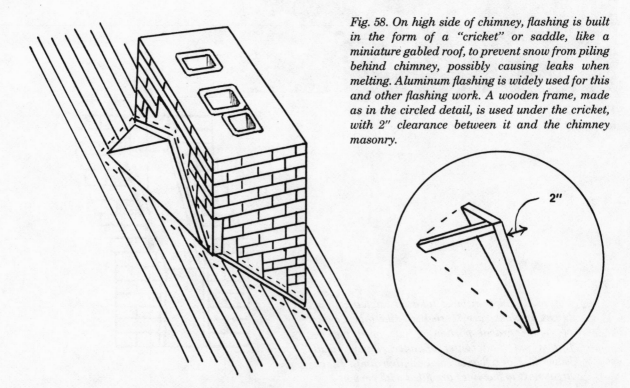

Fig. 58. On high side of chimney, flashing is built in the form of a "cricket" or saddle, like a miniature gabled roof, to prevent snow from piling behind chimney, possibly causing leaks when melting. Aluminum flashing is widely used for this and other flashing work. A wooden frame, made as in the circled detail, is used under the cricket, with 2″ clearance between it and the chimney masonry.

sonry, its location in the masonry may determine the procedure. In the fireplace in the step-by-step photos, the oil burner flue that comes up from the basement through the masonry is entirely outside of the house, hence not in close proximity to the wall framing. Where flues are inside, the sides of the fireplace are essentially indoor chimneys, and must be treated as such. One reason for maintaining chimney clearances lies in the possibility of overfiring or very prolonged firing. During a spell of unusually cold weather, for example, the fire in a fireplace may be maintained at a higher level than usual and for a longer time. The central heating system may also run overtime. Under these circumstances, a chimney that might have a good margin of safety under normal conditions could reach a hazardous surface temperature. A "chimney fire" caused by soot or creosote igniting in the chimney flue can produce the same type of overtemperature at the masonry surface. So, to play safe, it pays to go "overboard" somewhat on masonry thickness and correct clearance. Where the chimney passes through the roof, the 2″ clearance is maintained, and made waterproof by means of metal flashing applied as shown in the drawings. (See figs. 57 and 58.) Other flashing methods are also used. In all, the flashing is installed in such a way as to carry rainwater away from the chimney surface and onto the roof. As the aluminum flashing now commonly used (available from hardware and building suppliers) is very soft, it can be cut and formed easily to the required shapes.

Fig. 59. Aluminum flashing between roof and chimney looks like this. If you mount TV antenna on the chimney, the pole should be grounded by heavy copper or aluminum wire leading as directly as possible to underground metal water pipe or other effective grounding means, such as deep-driven grounding rod. NFPA requires grounding conductor not smaller than No. 10 copper wire or No. 8 aluminum. Check your local code requirements.

Fig. 60. When flashing is used at vertical wall-chimney juncture, it is sometimes bent out onto brickwork like this, depending on local code requirements.

CORNER AND ADJOINING-ROOM FIREPLACES

Fireplaces can be built in inside corners of a room like a peis or in an outside corner. They can also be built through a wall between rooms, so a single fireplace serves two separate areas. To avoid the possibility of occasional smoky operation, however, the outside corner and between-room types should have unimpeded draft, preferably a fairly tall chimney. Any cross draft through the room areas, caused by opening doors or by other air movements, creates a greater chance of moving the rising smoke out of the fireplace if the draft is at all sluggish. And the between-rooms fireplace should not be regarded as a means of heating two rooms, as there is no fireplace back to reflect heat into either one. Instead, think of it as a cheerful and novel conversation piece adding to the decor and providing some warmth for those seated near it.

Fig. 61. For modern effect you can build with masonry block. Front corner of this peis-styled fireplace is supported on short lally column available from building suppliers. Portland Cement Association.

Fig. 62. To save work you can build a masonry block fireplace and use a factory-made chimney, like this. Readymade fittings are available for attaching factory-made chimneys to masonry fireplaces. Portland Cement Association.

Fig. 63. This short masonry chimney has been extended with a factory-made Metlvent chimney for better draft with a wood stove.

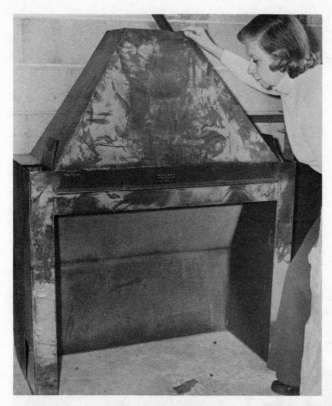

Fig. 64. *If you buy a factory-made circulating fireplace unit the proportions are automatically set for you. Just lay the masonry around the metal form according to the manufacturer's instructions. This one is a Heat Saver.*

Fig. 65. *If you want to build an inexpensive chimney with as little work as possible (in masonry) you can use chimney blocks like these. Large center opening is sized to fit square flue liner tiles. Just cement one block on top of the other, inserting and end-cementing flue tile liners as you go.*

CIRCULATING FIREPLACES

This is the masonry fireplace form that does the best heating job. You buy a readymade steel unit around which to build the circulating fireplace and you not only get more efficient heating but also easier construction. Although the details vary among makes and models, the general procedure is about the same. You build your foundation up to hearth level, then set your metal circulating unit on the hearth. To finish the job you build the masonry around it. In most cases, this eliminates all temporary forms for shaping the masonry, as the steel shell of the unit serves as the form for the masonry. Your fireplace size and smoke chamber shape are taken care of automatically, and you should use chimney block and flue size to match. You'll still need the lengths of steel angle, however, to support the fireplace facing and chimney above it. But, in most cases, your damper will be built into the metal circulating unit. Don't be surprised if the sides of your fireplace's metal inner shell are not splayed

Fig. 66. As these chimney blocks do not provide wall thickness necessary for building chimney against the house wall (if combustible) you build the chimney away from the wall and connect it with an approved connector pipe, as shown.

*Fig. 67. Impressive outdoor broilers can be built
from standard cement masonry block, like this,
along with standard block surfacing for patio.
Portland Cement Association.*

outward toward the front, as in the usual masonry type. They're more likely to be at right angles to the back. As the circulating design provides much more room-heating efficiency, the reflective effect of the splayed sides is not as essential, and the squared layout provides more log space at the rear. If you plan to use a circulating fireplace unit, look it (and the manufac-

turer's instructions) over in advance at the masonry or building suppliers where you'll buy it, and plan your job accordingly. Hot air ducts from it can feed heating air from the front or sides, or, in many models, to other rooms on the same floor or the floor above. Some models can also be fitted with a factory-made blower to distribute heated air to almost any part of the house.

Fig. 68. Using concrete blocks for foundation, chimney blocks for chimney, and stone or other decorative material for outer facing, you can make outdoor grille easily like this. Lengths of angle iron support chimney, as shown. Half-inch steel rods embedded in masonry of sides serve as support for food being cooked. Charcoal is the fuel.

Fig. 69. For the quickest, inexpensive masonry broiler job, you can buy ready-made blocks from masonry suppliers, designed to fit together "dry." A metal grille is also available from the same supplier. It can be used without cementing. Just take it apart if you want to move it and reassemble at new location. Large masonry suppliers stock various forms.

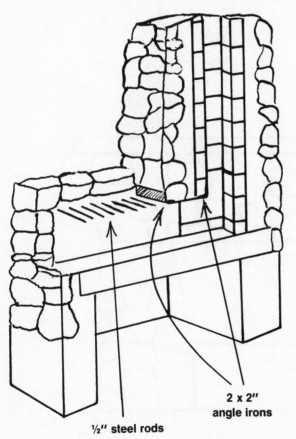

½" steel rods

**2 x 2"
angle irons**

Fig. 70. If you want a true Dutch oven you can build with an extra flue, like this. If you burn charcoal in it you can support food on an open mesh grille above the charcoal. If you want to burn wood in it, seal off the oven chamber with a metal bottom and connect flue to firebox below it where wood is burned. You can buy iron doors for the oven and the fire chamber below it, but may have to order them in advance. Favor a fire door with draft adjuster slide or disk.

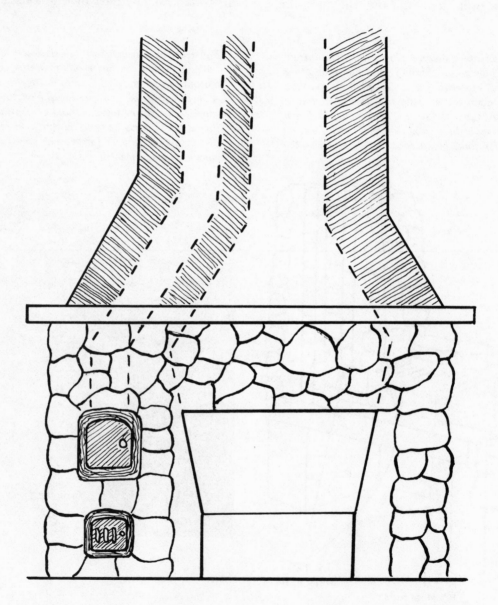

4

HOW TO BUY AND INSTALL A FACTORY-MADE CHIMNEY AND FIREPLACE

You can install an approved factory-made chimney for your fireplace or wood stove (or your oil burner) in as little as one day, sometimes even less. The specific working time depends on the situation. The chimney job shown for the potbelly stove was completed in five hours' working time, as it followed the simplest route—straight up through the roof of the enclosed porch. The one for the antique parlor stove required about eight hours, as its path led through the wall of the ground floor dining room, then up the outside of the house. Like conventional masonry chimneys, the factory-made ones can also be led up inside the house through floors and roof, but thanks to their light weight they can be supported entirely by the house structure and require no masonry foundation. A 30" length of a typical 7" inside diameter factory-made chimney, for example, weighs only 22 lbs., though a comparable height of masonry chimney might easily weigh close to 400 lbs. So, from the do-it-yourself standpoint the factory-mades not only save time but eliminate a lot of heavy work.

Fig. 71. Metlvent factory-made chimney (used in installation pictures) of 7" inside diameter weighs only 22 lbs. per 30" section length. It's made in inside diameters from 6-14", lengths from 6-30". In 6" diameter weight of 30" length is 19 lbs., in 14" diameter, 43 lbs. This type has inner and outer walls of stainless steel, high efficiency insulation between walls.

TYPES OF FACTORY-MADE CHIMNEYS

Factory-made chimneys are manufactured in two general types. One consists of an inner and outer metal pipe with special insulation between them. The Metlvent all-fuel chimney shown in the step-by-step installation photos is this type. Both the inner pipe, which is the flue, and the outer pipe that forms the protective shell, are of stainless steel in this brand. Thermagard ® insulation in the 1″ space between the pipes is locked in each section by the metal ends that enclose the unit.

The other chimney type utilizes air-cooling in a form of convection air circulation commonly called thermo-siphoning. This type consists of three concentric metal pipes with air space between them. The smoke and hot gases from the fire rise inside the innermost pipe, which is the flue. Heat conducted through the walls of the flue raises the temperature of the air in the space between the flue and the central pipe causing it also to rise and exit through the open end of that space at the top of the chimney. Replacement air from outside is drawn into the open top of the next space outward—the space between the central pipe and the outermost pipe. It travels *down* that space, cooling the outermost pipe as it goes, before passing *under the bottom* of the central pipe (through a base fitting made for the purpose), then up the space between the central pipe and the flue pipe to exit at the top, as previously described. This cooling flow, down the outer space and up the inner space continues as long as there's a fire to provide the heat for thermo-siphoning. The chimney top is designed with the cold air inlet below the hot air and flue outlets, with an intervening overhang that prevents hot air from being

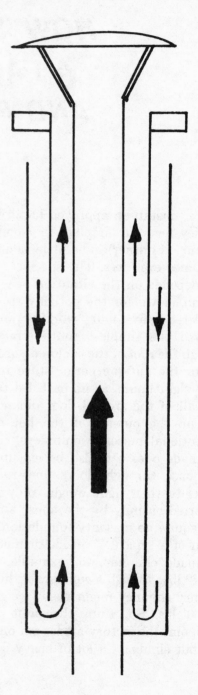

Fig. 72. Thermo-siphon air cooled type factory-made chimney has three walls, with air circulating between them, as in diagram. This type is sold in sections like insulated type, can be installed in similar manner.

drawn in with the cold air. The shingled and wood-paneled chimneys shown in the photos (see figs. 73 and 74) enclose Majestic thermo-siphoning chimneys. The flue pipe of these is stainless steel, the central pipe aluminized steel, and the outer pipe galvanized steel.

CHIMNEY HEIGHT AND DIAMETER

Either type of chimney can easily be assembled in the height required for almost any private home. A single support can carry 65′ of the insulated Metlvent chimney shown. Flue supports at 30′ intervals are used with the thermo-siphoning one illustrated. Total maximum height can be up to 90′. The diameter of the flue should be at least as large as that of the flue fitting of the heating unit it is to serve. (In the case of a fireplace, the cross-sectional area of the flue should not be less than $\frac{1}{12}$ the area of the fireplace opening. If you plan to buy a factory-made fireplace, however, you may find a matched factory-made chimney is available for it from the same manufacturer.) In general, because of the possibility of soot or other combustion products accumulating on the inside surface of the flue, you may find the flue size is somewhat larger than the minimum required, especially with lower chimney heights.

Both of the factory-made chimney types can be offset (rather than straight all the way) by means of angled fittings where necessary to avoid framing members of the house structure, or to penetrate the roof closer to the ridge, when the chimney route is inside the house. A simulated brick or plain housing may be used with either type chimney where it emerges from the roof.

(See fig. 97.) If the chimney is mounted outside the house, either type may be enclosed in a wood-framed structure (called a "chase") like those in the photos. (See figs. 73 and 74.) To save time, however, the insulated chimney shown in fig. 99 was left exposed. The stainless steel withstands weathering, and can be enclosed at any time, if desired. Both types can also be used with conventional masonry fireplaces as well as with factory-made ones, and wood stoves or central heating units.

HOW TO BUY A FACTORY-MADE CHIMNEY

A little preliminary planning and checking is essential before you buy your chimney. First, be sure the brand of chimney you plan to use has been tested and approved by a recognized testing organization. (Those shown in this chapter are listed by UL.) Next, check your local building code for any special regulations concerning chimneys. The chances are they'll follow those of the National Fire Protection Association. These require that the chimney extend at least 3′ above the high side of the roof opening through which it passes, and that it be at least 2′ higher than any portion of the house that's within 10′ of it, horizontally. This, of course, includes any portion of the roof.

If the chimney is to be used with a wood stove, you should also decide on the particular wood stove you're going to buy before the job begins, as this may affect the location of the chimney. Certain types of wood stoves, for example, must be located farther from combustible room walls than other types, as shown by the diagram in

Fig. 73. Either insulated or thermo-siphoning factory-made chimneys can be enclosed in a wood-framed "chase" and shingled like this one on newly built New England home. Chimney serves fireplace. Conventional masonry foundation at this location (above garage) would not be feasible, as it would block space required for garage doors.

Fig. 74. Another form of wooden chase, using vertical T&G boards to match house. In this one, fireplace is set in living room wall above inner end of garage. As no foundation is needed for fireplace or chimney, no space is taken from garage area.

Chapter 5 (see fig. 113). Use this diagram to determine the permissible locations for the stove you plan to buy. It is also important to know the basic type of chimney you'll use and the flue diameter you'll require. This determines the outside diameter of the chimney and whether it will fit between house framing members like joists and rafters without requiring alteration work to provide the necessary clearance.

The usual minimum clearance (open space) required between the outside surface of the chimney and any combustible material, such as the wood in the house structure, is 2″, which also applies to masonry chimneys in most situations. (More than one factory-made chimney may also be used in a single chase, just as several flues may be built into a conventional masonry chimney. But the required clearance to combustible materials in the chase must be maintained. If a factory-made chimney is to be used in a chase, also check in advance with the manufacturer's specifications as to whether the enclosed space must be ventilated. If so, use the method or fitting specified for the purpose.) Use only factory-made parts and fittings, no homemade makeshifts. And *don't* mix brands.

FACTS ABOUT AN OUTSIDE CHIMNEY

Although factory-made chimneys can be installed either inside or outside of the house, the outside installation is often the easiest for the do-it-yourselfer. The chimney is simply led out through the house wall at the starting point, then straight up the outside wall. No passages through ceilings, floors or roof are involved. (Make sure in advance, however, that the chimney you

plan to install can be used in the way you want to use it.) Thermo-siphoning types are usually enclosed in a chase, though insulated types, like the Metlvent used in the installation examples, are often left exposed to get the heating unit in operation as quickly as possible. They can, of course, be enclosed at any time. (Inside installations are described later.)

INSTALLING AN OUTSIDE CHIMNEY

If you'll be doing the work yourself, be sure you're familiar with the assembly procedures before you actually start the job. Once you've bought the chimney sections and fittings needed for the route your chimney is to take, make a trial fit-together of the parts you'll be using. It's easier to get the knack on the ground than on a ladder.

The first step in the job itself is making the wall opening for the chimney. It must be at the proper height for stove or free-standing fireplace you'll use. For smaller sizes, like the 7″ flue diameter chimney shown in the step-by-step photos, the wall opening is merely a square hole cut between the studs (posts) inside the wall. These are usually spaced 16″ apart from the center of one to the center of the next one. You can locate them by tapping the wall lightly with a hammer. It sounds and feels more solid at the stud locations. You can also buy several types of "stud locater" at most hardware stores. When you've selected the between-stud space where your chimney opening is to be, take a look at it from the basement. If plumbing runs up through the same space you'll avoid complications by using another space for your chimney opening. Shifting plumbing

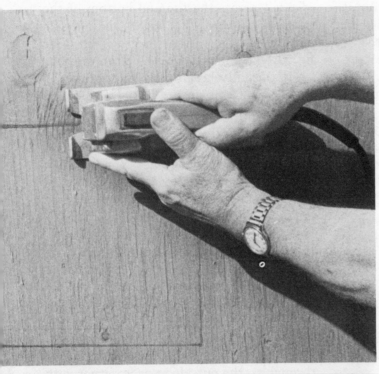

Fig. 75. First step in thru-wall factory-made chimney installation job is cutting through wall. Hole size must match square firestop spacer required for wall pass-through. Job starts inside, as in text, then outside wall is cut, as shown. Sabre saw makes job easy.

Fig. 76. Firestop spacer has flanges on inner side (shown) so it can't be mounted with round chimney hole too close to any side. Flanges fit inside wall framing members.

around is usually a complicated job. If there's wiring in the space it's easier to relocate. But avoid this extra work, too, if you can. For either type of shift, you may need a permit, depending on your local code. Wall frame alterations can also frequently solve this type of problem.

As the 2 x 4 studs are actually only 1½" thick, the space between their facing surfaces is 14½". So you cut a 14½" square opening in the wall, and toenail a crosspiece

Fig. 77. If chimney outside diameter is small enough to fit between framing members (like studs) with required clearance, no framing alteration is needed. In studding, drive nails into studs as at "A" just above and below the opening cut through the inside wallboard. Leave half the nail length protruding. These nails act as "stops" to hold the horizontal crosspieces while you drive toe nails "B". Without the stop-nails it's more difficult to drive the toe nails that hold the crosspieces.

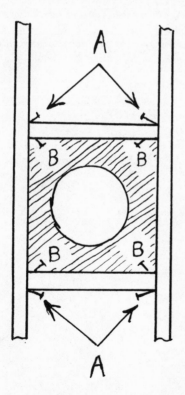

of 2 x 4 across the top and bottom of the opening between the inside and outside surfaces of the wall, as diagrammed. (See fig. 77.) This makes a firm rim all around.

It's usually best to cut the opening in the interior wall surface first. Use a pencil to outline the square to be cut. Then, with an icepick or an awl, make three or four closely spaced holes through the wallboard along one of the pencil lines. You can then use a pointed knife to join the holes to make a starting slot for any small pointed hand saw, like a compass saw. From there, you can cut all the way around the outlined square, and finally remove the cut-out piece. An electric sabre saw, of course, can do the job faster, but you may end up having to replace the blade, as gypsum board tends to dull fast-moving wood-cutting blades.

Once the inside hole is cut, you can drill through to the outside at each corner with about a ⅛" diameter drill. By joining these holes with a pencil line, you have a perfectly matched cutting outline for sabre-sawing the outside wall surface, as shown in fig. 75. You can make the starting slot by drilling a ⅜" hole inside two diagonally opposite corners. From these holes, you can cut the entire square. You finish the opening by nailing a metal "firestop spacer" to the 2 x 4 rim on both the interior and exterior surfaces of the wall. Each spacer (manufactured for the chimney) has a round, chimney-size hole centered in it to hold the chimney permanently at an even distance from the wood around it. As the chimney in the step-by-step photos has an outside diameter of 9", this provides a clearance of 2¾" on all sides—safely in excess of the required 2". The protruding inner rim riveted to the firestop spacer (see figs. 76 and 78) faces inside the wall and

Fig. 78. Firestop spacer is mounted with flanges "in."

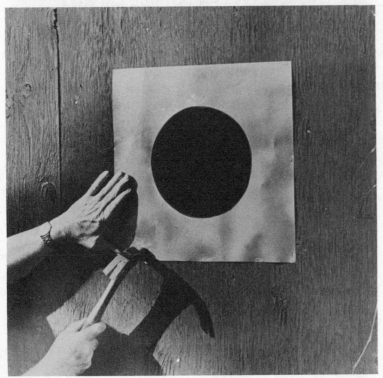

Fig. 79. Spacer is nailed to outer wall surface. Another one is nailed to inner wall surface, in matching position.

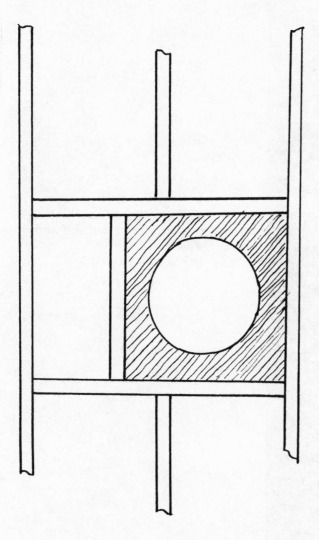

Fig. 80. If the outside diameter of the chimney is too large for the space between framing members, cut one of the studs (or joists, if it's floor framing) and add crosspieces like this, nailed firmly where cross members join existing framing. Then add additional member to square in chimney opening. Job requires removing area of inner wallboard.

prevents the spacer from being installed incorrectly, with the chimney too close to any side of the opening. The spacers, of course, are bought to match the chimney size. If you use a chimney too large to fit between studs with the required clearance, you'll have to cut a larger wall opening and alter the framework around it, as shown in fig. 80. You remove a section of one stud and use crosspieces nailed to its remaining ends to span the space between the next stud on each side. You can then place the final opening anywhere in the rimmed area. The same method also lets you locate your wall opening where a stud would ordinarily interfere. This is sometimes necessary when there's little or no leeway in the stove's location.

ASSEMBLING AN OUTSIDE CHIMNEY

The section of chimney that runs through the wall and the firestop spacers must be long enough to extend (when connected) from the insulated T outside to a point slightly inside the interior wall. A stovepipe adapter fitting connects to the interior end to take the single walled smoke pipe from the stove or free-standing fireplace. The outer end connects to the insulated T that starts the vertical run of the chimney. The metal wall support, lag-screwed to the outside house wall (if wall is wood) supports the T and up to 45′ of vertical chimney above it. To be sure the horizontal through-the-wall section of chimney aligns with its connection to the T, assemble the T on its wall support and connect it to the horizontal chimney section, with a helper holding the T in place while you drive the first lag screws.

Fig. 81. Wall support bracket (for through-wall chimneys) goes on next. It can be used with braces below, as shown, or with them above (inverted) if situation requires. Nail it temporarily to permit adjustment, if necessary.

Fig. 82. Starter and cleanout T is mounted on wall support bracket. Short, through-wall chimney section fits into it. All chimney fittings are stainless steel, support is galvanized.

How to Buy and Install a Factory-made Chimney and Fireplace   85

Fig. 83. Starter T mounted. Slip rings will be tapped into place to lock all sections of chimney pipe together.

From this point on, the assembly job is just a matter of connecting successive sections of chimney to make up the total vertical portion. Be sure, however, that the chimney sections have the correct end up. You'll find an arrow and the word "up" embossed on the outer shell of each Metl-vent section, usually also on other brands. You don't have to turn or twist the Metl-vent sections to lock them together. You simply stack each section on the upper end of the one below it, and slide the slip ring (supplied with each section) over the locking tabs in the lower end of each section. (The upper end of the lower section fits into the lower end of the upper one.) The ring forces the tabs into the locking groove around the upper end of the lower section. You can use a wood block to tap the ring into locking position. (The sections can be disassembled by reversing the process.)

A "wall band" matched to the chimney diameter is used to hold the chimney to the wall at 8′ intervals. The band and its bracket automatically maintain the proper clearance between chimney and wall. If the chimney must clear a fascia board or other part extending outward beyond the wall, the wall band brackets and the T support must be mounted on blocks to provide the added clearance needed, as shown in figs. 86 and 87. This extra clearance should be figured in advance, as the length of the horizontal section of chimney (through the wall) must be planned accordingly.

If the chimney extends 5′ or more above the roof it must be braced by metal struts running from the chimney to the roof. They are attached to a support band around the chimney, similar to the wall bands.

Fig. 84. *Soot pocket and drip-cleanout at base of starter T (hand is on it) can be removed easily for cleaning. It keeps chimney clear, prevents rain that may enter chimney top from reaching stove or other heating appliance.*

Fig. 85. *Fingers hold locking slip ring which, here, has been tapped into locking position. It locks first section of chimney to starter T.*

Fig. 87. Completed chimney with chimney "topper" to keep out rain. Note that chimney clears roof by 36″, is also 24″ higher than any portion of building within 10′.

Fig. 86. Wall support, T and first section of chimney assembled. Wall band holds chimney section to wall. Spacer blocks of wood are used under support bracket and wall band attachment points to bring chimney out far enough from wall to clear fascia board by required distance.

*Fig. 88. Inside house, single walled flue connector
from antique wood stove connects to through-wall
section of factory-made chimney. Traditional flue
pipe collar covers starter fitting of chimney.*

Fig. 89. Similar installation using full ceiling height brick panel, with stove resting on flagstone over sheet metal wood floor protection.

INSTALLING AN INSIDE CHIMNEY

If your chimney is to pass up through the inside of the house the installation steps in the job are much the same, except that you cut the openings in the ceiling and roof rather than in the wall, and you use fittings made for the purpose. You start by cutting an opening in the ceiling, between ceiling joists instead of between wall studs. If any framing alteration is necessary to accommodate the chimney size, you follow the same general plan as diagrammed for studs, but you use lumber matched to the joist size or rafter size.

The first fitting, called a ceiling support, not only carries the weight of the chimney,

Fig. 90. Ceiling starter support for type of factory-made chimney shown in photos, is installed from below rafters. Upper portion is then ready for first chimney section. Round metal collar of support has pre-punched holes for nailing directly to framing, after adding crosspieces between framing members. Follow manufacturer's instructions.

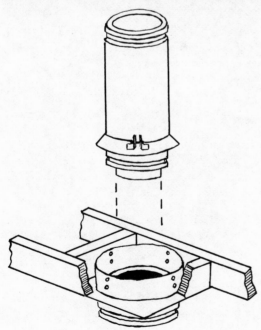

but also provides the proper clearance to combustibles. It's made with an outer metal sleeve that you nail directly to the framing (with 2½" common nails) through factory-drilled holes. If the sleeve doesn't fit snugly against the frame members on all four sides, you modify the framing to get the snug fit. It's a simple matter, of course, to place the crosspieces between joists to provide this fit. If the joists are almost close enough, you may be able to do the trick there by nailing wood shim pieces to their facing surfaces to fill the gap.

Put the support fitting in place from the underside of the framed opening. Then drive one nail *part way* into the framing through one of the factory-drilled holes in each side of the sleeve, This way, you can check the fitting's position (to make sure it's not tilted) and pull and re-drive the nails if any correction is needed before final nailing. If all's well, drive nails all the way through all of the holes provided.

The "cone collar" that comes with the support goes on the lower end of the first section of the chimney, tightened into the groove at the section's lower end. After the collar is snugged in place, you lower the chimney section into the support from the top, making sure it's well seated in the pocket provided in the support. Once it's in place, you can stack other sections on top of it, fastening them to each other by sliding the slip rings into locking position. If you can't slide the rings into place with finger pressure, use a wood block to tap them into place. (You can dismantle assembled sections by reversing the procedure—tapping the slip rings back up the chimney section to release the locking tabs.) Wherever the chimney passes through a floor or ceiling above the starting one, you use a ceiling firestop spacer (dif-

Fig. 91. *If factory-made chimney must go through ceiling, job starts like this. Here, panel of dropped ceiling on enclosed porch has been removed. Holes are being drilled up through corners of opening location for ceiling type firestop spacer. Where holes emerge through roof, they will be used to outline the opening, so sabre saw can cut downward to make opening, as in next photo. You work inside, from stepladder.*

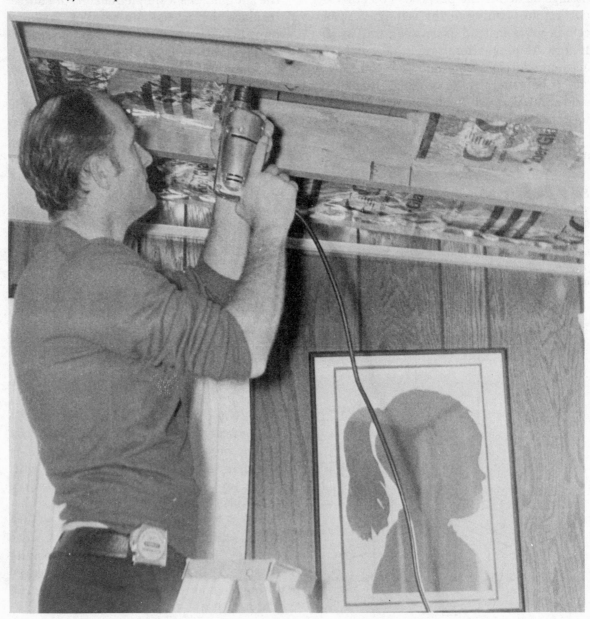

Fig. 92. Roof job. Here, undersized hole is cut first. This lets you actually see where you're cutting when you make hole full sized, prevents accidental cutting into roof rafters. Use coarse-toothed wood cutting blade. It minimizes clogging from composition shingles.

How to Buy and Install a Factory-made Chimney and Fireplace 93

Fig. 93. After full-sized hole is cut, ceiling support is nailed into framing. This is mounted level, so chimney will stand vertically on it. It's made so you can't make a mistake. Correct clearance to wood framing is provided automatically by design of support. Nail holes are pre-drilled at factory.

Fig. 94. With chimney supported through roof hole by support fitting, adjustable flashing is slipped over it, like this.

Fig. 95. Flashing has been roof-cemented to seal it around edges. Storm collar has been mounted around chimney a few inches above top of flashing unit. The collar will be slipped down to close flashing, and tightened in place with screw provided. Chimney cap keeps out rain.

ferent from a wall-type spacer) to automatically provide the required clearance to combustible framing.

At the roof, the procedure depends on the arrangement you select for terminating your chimney. If you use a squared housing in plain or simulated brick finish, follow the assembly instructions for the brand you're using. Some are made up of fit-together sides, assembled on the spot. Others are complete box-type units. A "flashing" method is provided for all of them, to prevent rain from leaking under the base. The flashing is simply a metal apron designed to seal the roof-chimney juncture and direct rain flow away from the chimney base.

If you want the simplest chimney termination you can cap the chimney with a rain hood called a "topper" in the brand illustrated. This roofs over the upper end of the chimney and prevents rain from entering. You seal the chimney-roof juncture with a factory-made flashing fitting that can be adjusted to suit the roof pitch, as in figs. 94 and 95. Then tighten a storm collar (similar to the starting cone collar) just above the top of the flashing, using MV sealer tape to seal the storm collar to the chimney to prevent rain seepage, but you *do not* caulk the flashing to the chimney. Spacer clips in the top opening of the flashing automatically set the collar position to provide ventilation to avoid heat build-up at the chimney top. If you don't use some sort of rain shield over the chimney top you need a starter T and drip cap at the bottom, so rain entering the chimney won't run into your stove or fireplace. Your best bet, however, is a rain shield suited to the type of chimney termination you select.

Fig. 96. Inside, this chimney connects to single-walled flue connector pipe from potbelly stove. Here, finishing touches are completed on the flagstone that protects wood floor under stove. Entire job, with stove in operation, was completed in less than a weekend.

Fig. 97. If you want masonry effect on factory-made chimney that emerges through roof, you can use a simulated brick chimney "termination" like this one, which is made for a Majestic thermo-siphon type. Similar ones are made for insulated types.

INSTALLING A FACTORY-MADE EXTENSION ON A MASONRY CHIMNEY

If you have an existing masonry chimney that's too short for good performance, you can increase its height with minimum effort by using factory-made chimney sections to extend it. You use a "fireplace anchor plate" (usually used to start a factory-made fireplace chimney from a masonry fireplace) to start your chimney extension from the prepared top of your existing masonry chimney. This a flat plate with a short, centered section of chimney in it, and pre-drilled holes in the plate corners. Bolts firmly embedded head down in the masonry of the chimney top, and spaced to match the plate holes, provide the anchors for the chimney. Leave enough of the threaded portion above the concrete for fastening. You can stack the number of sections you need from there up; use bracing if an exposed factory-made chimney extends more than 5' above its starting point. Two braces are needed.

Electrical conduit, available from electrical supply dealers, is well suited to use as a bracing of this type. If the conduit is steel you can use it in ¾" diameter. If aluminum, the diameter should be the next size larger. The best angle for the brace is about 45 degrees to the chimney, though it can vary within reasonable limits. You can determine the length of the braces by holding the conduit with one end at the point where it will attach to the building, and the other alongside the chimney where it will attach to the support band. Hacksaw the conduit slightly over-length to allow for flattening an inch or so at each end. The flattened ends at the support band around the chimney should be vertical, the ends attaching to the roof, at right angles to those at the chimney. This way, the bolts run directly through one flattened end into the support band, and lag screws run directly through the other flattened end into the roof. To avoid the possibility of leaks it's wise to bed the roof end in roofing cement before tightening down the lag screws. Drill $\frac{7}{32}''$ holes for the bolts into the support band. Drill the other ends for $\frac{1}{4}''$ lag screws about $1\frac{1}{2}''$ long for the usual shingled roof with plywood roof decking under the shingles.

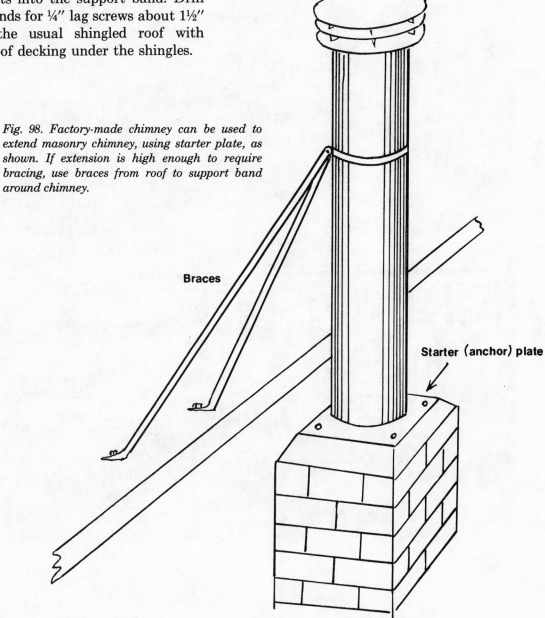

Fig. 98. Factory-made chimney can be used to extend masonry chimney, using starter plate, as shown. If extension is high enough to require bracing, use braces from roof to support band around chimney.

Braces

Starter (anchor) plate

Fig. 99. On a one-and-a-half story house, this Metlvent chimney is left exposed, painted to match trim. Blocks hold wall bands out from wall for proper clearance at fascia board (barge board).

Fig. 100. Inside house shown in preceding photo, chimney connects to this fireplace stove. Brick panel shields wall, stove rests on large flagstone slab supported on masonry blocks.

How to Buy and Install a Factory-made Chimney and Fireplace   101

FACTORY-MADE FIREPLACES

Today, you can buy a tested and approved factory-made fireplace either in circulating or non-circulating form, designed for *zero clearance*. This means that it can be installed on a wood floor or subfloor, and in actual contact with the wood framing of the house. It's not a fireplace stove but a full-fledged fireplace that looks exactly like the traditional type. And you can finish it with anything from brick to marble. As the photos show, you can't tell the completed job from its conventional masonry counterparts. Yet no masonry foundation is required. The fireplace and its factory-made chimney together are light enough to be supported by the house structure.

Typically, the zero clearance is made possible by high temperature insulation, reflective metal, a special refractory hearth and firebox liner, and convection air cooling. As the specifics vary with the make and model, however, you follow the installation instructions that come with the brand you buy. And, in most cases, you use only a factory-made chimney matched to the fireplace by the manufacturer.

Fig. 101. You can't tell a factory-made fireplace from one built-in by traditional methods. This is a Majestic Thulman model designed for zero-clearance and is suited to formal decor. It's used with Majestic thermo-siphon-cooled factory-made chimney.

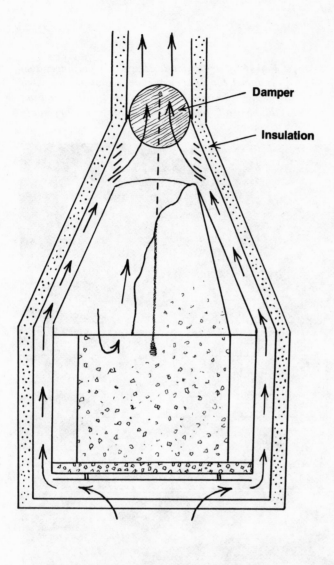

Damper

Insulation

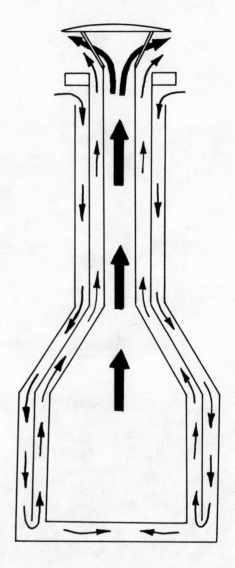

Fig. 103. When zero-clearance factory-made fireplace is used with insulated type factory-made chimney (like the Heatilator shown in fig. 102) cooling air flows in under fireplace bottom and under top of fireplace opening into cooling channels that rise up front, sides and back. Cooling air flow is drawn into flue through louvers just below damper, and rises up chimney with flue gases. Chain closes damper and can be held in clip fitting at any intermediate setting. When chain is released, weight on one side of damper causes it to open. Refractory material lines fireplace bottom and back. For clarity, some of the metal heat shields are not shown.

Fig. 104. Air flow pattern through a Majestic fireplace and matching thermo-siphon-cooled chimney. As heat from fire rises in flue, heat is transferred to air passage next to flue, causing air in that passage to rise and exit at chimney top, as shown. It is replaced by cold air drawn into outer passage, which flows downward, cooling outer shell of chimney and fireplace. This air flows under intermediate wall at bottom, as shown, then rises and exits. Cooling flow is continuous while fire is going.

If possible, read the installation instructions for the fireplace you plan to buy, before you buy it. If you're buying from a local supplier he may have a set of instructions you can read while you're there. This can save work later and eliminate confusion, as installation procedures may vary widely with make and model for practical reasons. The instructions may, for example, call for setting the fireplace in position with a starter section of chimney on it *before* the upper portion of the chimney is installed. This makes it easier to mark accurately for the chimney opening in the ceiling. Since the fireplace is permanently fitted into the house structure it can't be shifted like a wood stove to make up for a miscalculated chimney location.

INSTALLATION AND PRELIMINARIES

Plan your installation completely, before the job begins. You can get the information you need, including fireplace sizes and chimney dimensions and assembly methods from the supplier from whom you'll buy your unit. The one shown in the installation photos (see figs. 106-109) is a Heatilator with a front opening 38″ wide and 26½″ high. The fireplace is approved for zero clearance, the chimney for 2″ clearance. As the outside of the double-walled insulated chimney section is 14″, this means that the openings through which the chimney passes at ceilings, floors or roof, must be 18 x 18″. Metal firestop spacers made for this size opening are used for holding the chimney at the required clearance at ceilings and floors. (If the chimney is offset at an angle along part of its run to avoid parts of the house structure or emerge at a particular roof location,

rectangular spacers are available to provide the correct spacing at pass-through points.) A hearth extension of approved noncombustible material at least ⅜″ thick is required to protect a combustible floor (like a wooden one) for at least 16″ in front of the fireplace opening, and 8″ to each side. (Larger hearth extensions are required for larger fireplace openings.) And a minimum clearance of 3′ must be provided from the fireplace opening to any combustible wall that projects at 90 degrees from the plane of the fireplace opening. For example, if the fireplace is in a wall near a corner, at no point must its opening be closer than 3′ to the adjoining wall. It may, however, be installed at 45 degrees across a room corner.

THE CHIMNEY PATH

As the fireplace chimney must pass through the ceiling above the fireplace location, check over the ceiling framing in advance of the actual installation work. This is a simple matter if the ceiling is under an unfloored attic. As the ceiling joists are likely to be 16″ apart (center to center), you'll probably have to cut one of them and "box" the 18″ square opening for the chimney, as shown for walls in fig. 80. You can plan this ahead of time, though the actual work is best done after the fireplace is set in the position it will occupy, as described shortly.

TO START THE JOB

When your fireplace arrives check the carton in which it's delivered to be sure all the parts are in it. This is also a good time to try the damper so you'll know how to

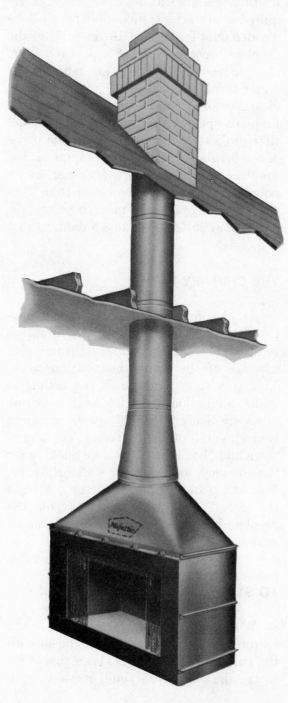

Fig. 105. Thermo-siphoning chimney passage through floor and roof, from fireplace to chimney termination. Factory-made chimney shown is a Majestic.

operate it. (In the model shown, it's open when the handle is up, closed when the handle is down.) It's also wise to review the installation instructions even if you've already read them. Many instructions are clearer when you can look at the parts to which they apply.

The first step in the job is mounting the starter section of chimney on top of the fireplace and setting the fireplace in the location you've planned for it. A helper is very handy at this stage. Then you can use a plumb line or carpenter's level and straight edge to mark the ceiling so you can make the boxed opening directly above the center of the chimney starting point on the fireplace. If there's enough headroom in the attic it may be easier to cut the joist from there, though you'll have to cut the ceiling opening first in most cases, to provide working room for the saw. (As only one joist need be cut in most instances, you'll probably find it easiest with a hand saw.) Nail scrap wood temporarily across the joists to be cut and the adjacent ones to provide support during the cutting, and until the headers are nailed in place to box the opening.

Unless the fireplace will be held firmly in position by the wall framing, nail blocks to the floor against its base to prevent it from shifting. Once the fireplace is in place with the ceiling opening boxed, you add chimney sections to carry the chimney up through the opening. A firestop spacer (a manufactured part matched to the chimney) is used to hold it centered in the opening with the required clearance.

The procedure where the chimney passes through the roof depends on the type of "roof termination" you select. Complete instructions are shipped with each type of termination, however. In general, the roof

Fig. 106. First step after factory-made fireplace and chimney is delivered, is checking to make sure all parts are on hand. Also familiarize yourself with parts like damper, that won't be so easy to examine after unit is installed. Heatilator.

pass-through job will be similar to that at the ceiling, except that the parts used can be adjusted to the roof pitch and provide a watertight seal. As roof rafters are often farther apart than the ceiling joists (2′ spacing is common) you may be able to box the chimney opening without cutting a rafter. A little advance planning often makes this possible by a slight change in the planned fireplace location. The basic steps shown earlier in this chapter can serve as a general guide to the chimney work.

To develop the exact approach to your own job, examine the brand of chimney you'll be using, and the instructions that go with it. Your supplier can usually provide a set of instructions to help figure out the job in advance.

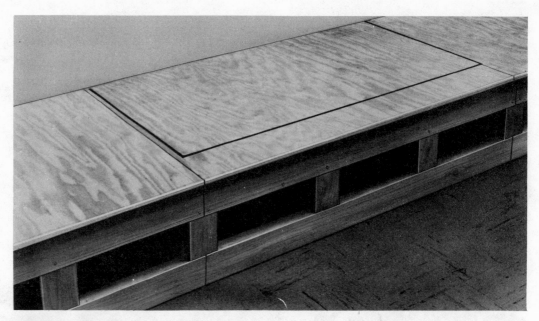

Fig. 107. If you want a raised hearth with a zero-clearance factory-made fireplace, all you have to do is build a plywood platform like this to support the fireplace above the floor level. Heatilator.

Fig. 108. Installation begins with setting of fireplace in location, and mounting first section of chimney. If it won't be locked in position by framing, nail blocks against base to hold it. Heatilator.

Fig. 109. Framing built around fireplace. In this example, fireplace would protrude from wall. It may also be recessed flush with wall. Chimney rises in center, elbowed heat-circulating ducts (to warm room) exit through sides of framed enclosure. Framing may run to ceiling. Framework is covered with gypsum wallboard. Fireplace may be trimmed as desired. Heatilator.

III

All About Wood Stoves

5

HOW TO BUY AND
INSTALL A WOOD STOVE

Select your wood stove to suit your own individual requirements. You know the job it has to do, and the style you want. The location of the stove, of course, is determined by the chimney location, old or new, and by the required clearance distance between the stove and the walls of the room. (More about this shortly.) The availability of the stove may also be a factor. Because of the high demand for wood stoves in general and certain models in particular, manufacturer's production is sometimes far behind incoming orders. So, unless you're willing to wait, you may have to compromise. The basic stove information that follows should help you not only to choose a stove that suits your particular situation but also to make a compromise if it proves necessary.

SPACE AND SAFETY FACTORS

The *kind* of stove you should buy determines how close it can be to a combustible wall (like the usual framed house wall)

and what kind of protection a combustible floor (like a wood floor) must have if the stove is to stand on it. When you know the rules, however, your stove choice is an easy matter, as true wood stoves are classified in only two general types. (Both are termed "room heaters" by fire and code people.)

Radiant type stoves consist of a single metal shell (technically called the heat exchanger) that contains the fire. Old familiar designs like the Franklin stove, log stove and the potbelly stove are radiant types. The heat of the fire is radiated directly into the room and to objects in the room. When the fire is brisk the radiant heat close to the stove can be intense enough to set combustible materials afire. So the National Fire Protection Association (NFPA) requires that radiant type stoves be placed no closer than 36 inches from any combustible wall.

Circulating type stoves consist of an inner metal shell (the heat exchanger) with the fire in it and an outer metal jacket an inch or so away from the inner shell. Openings at the top and bottom of the intervening space permit a constant up-

Fig. 110. Radiant *type wood stove, like this box stove for logs, consists of single metal shell with fire inside. Heat radiates directly from hot metal. This is the No. 38 Monitor model by Portland Stove Foundry, Inc., Portland, Maine.*

Fig. 111. Circulating *type wood stove here is a Sears Wonder Wood automatic. Fire is contained in inner heat exchanger, with metal outer cabinet. Non-electric thermostatic control lets you adjust heat level. Draft opens and closes as required to maintain level. Circulating stoves are also made without thermostatic control.*

ward flow of air by natural convection (hot air rising) whenever there's a fire in the stove. The flow of air carries the heat into the room, and the outer jacket blocks a major portion of the radiant heat that would otherwise reach nearby objects. So the NFPA allows this type of stove to be placed as close as 12″ from room walls at the sides and back. At the front, however, 24″ is required, or whatever distance is needed to take care of the fire and the stove maintenance. All this, assuming the stove is designed for tending from the front. (If the outer metal jacket has side or back openings in it that permit some direct radiation from the inner heat exchanger, the heater must be considered a radiant type.) Neither type of heater should be installed in an alcove because of the risk of heat build-up.

TO REDUCE CLEARANCES—SAFELY

If the required stove-to-wall space creates problems in the room layout, you can get by safely with less clearance *if you add special wall protection* specified by the NFPA. One of the simplest forms of this protection consists of sheet metal of at least 28-gauge thickness, mounted 1″ from the wall on noncombustible spacers, as shown in fig. 112. You can buy the metal from sheet metal suppliers. Look in your local Yellow Pages under "sheet metal." The same form of protection can be used to reduce single-wall stovepipe clearance distance from the wall or ceiling, as diagrammed. It is very important that the protection extends to each side of the stove or stovepipe for the same distance as that required when no protection is used.

Before you plan your installation, however, check the requirements of your local code, if your area has one. If it's available in printed form, buy a copy. If not, talk to your building inspector about your planned stove installation. As your local regulations have the force of law, they're the ones you have to follow, and they may differ somewhat from the ones outlined above.

FLOOR PROTECTION

If your stove (room heater) is mounted on legs that provide at least 4″ of open space between the stove bottom and the floor, you can use it on a combustible floor (like a wood floor) *if the floor is properly protected*. The minimum protection permitted by the NFPA under the stove is a layer of sheet metal of not less than 24 gauge thickness, extending at least 18″ beyond the stove at the front or side from which the ashes are removed. You may, of course, increase the area of the protection beyond the sides and back of the stove, and cover the metal with a layer of flagstone, slate, tile or other noncombustible material not only for added protection but also because it suits the decor of the room, as shown in figs. 116-118. Naturally, carpeting or other combustible floor covering must be removed from the area before the protection is applied. If you think you might later move the stove to another location, save the removed piece of floor covering. If you do the job carefully, you can replace the section with very little evidence that it was ever removed.

IN-THE-FIREPLACE STOVES

If you already have a non-circulating fireplace and would like to increase its heating efficiency without sacrificing the cheery glow of a visible log fire, there are several ways to do it. And you don't lose any floor space. One of the simplest is a wood stove designed for use *in the fireplace*. In its usual form, it's a rectangular log stove with screen or heat resistant glass in its doors. The flue pipe from the stove is led directly up to the fireplace flue above it, and sealed in the opening with an adapter plate that fits the damper opening. Installation is quick and easy. A damper in the stove itself takes the place of the fireplace damper. When the stove is in operation the smoke and combustion gases rise up the fireplace chimney while room air circulates by convection around the stove (between it and the inside walls of the fireplace), carrying stove heat into the room.

Another type of in-the-fireplace stove

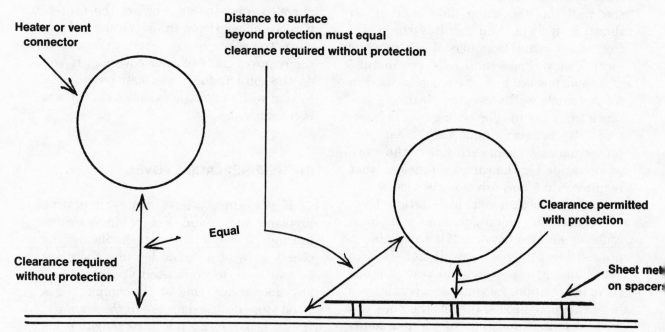

Heater or vent connector

Distance to surface beyond protection must equal clearance required without protection

Equal

Clearance required without protection

Clearance permitted with protection

Sheet metal on spacers

Combustible wall or ceiling

Fig. 112. By using 28 gauge sheet metal (or thicker) spaced out 1″ from wall or ceiling on noncombustible spacers, you can reduce the required clearance from a combustible wall or ceiling. If you use NFPA recommendations it works like this:

Where clearance without protection is 36″, protected clearance is:

Above	Sides and rear	Chimney or vent connector
18″	12″	18″

Where required clearance without protection is 18″, protected clearance is:

Above	Sides and rear	Chimney or vent connector
9″	6″	9″

Where required clearance without protection is 12″, protected clearance is:

Above	Sides and rear
6″	4″

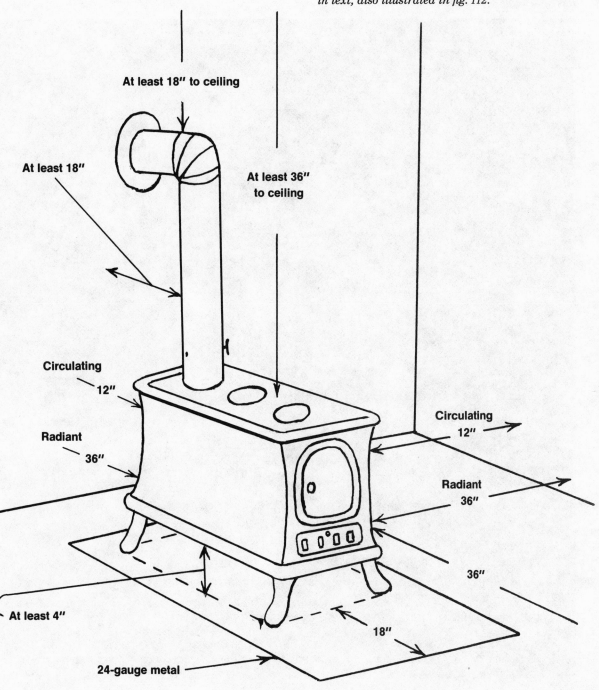

Fig. 113. Clearance distances from stove and flue connector pipe (single walled) and combustible walls and ceiling. Added protection makes possible reduction in clearance distance, as described in text, also illustrated in fig. 112.

At least 18″ to ceiling

At least 18″

At least 36″ to ceiling

Circulating
12″

Radiant
36″

Circulating
12″

Radiant
36″

36″

At least 4″

18″

24-gauge metal

Fig. 114. *In-the-fireplace stove connects to fireplace flue through damper opening, steals no floor space and converts ordinary fireplace to more efficient circulating type. Made in various sizes, it has adjustable panels to fit fireplace opening.*

Fig. 115. Installed in fireplace, the stove looks like this with glass doors closed. Air from the room enters through mesh at bottom and lower sides, and emerges from mesh higher up after being heated by stove. This one is El-Fuego III.

Fig. 116. A variation. Fireplace opening is covered by metal panel through which wood stove projects into room, with floor protection beyond front of existing hearth. Stove flue opens into fireplace, smoke rises through fireplace damper and up chimney. This one is Better 'n Ben's, by C & D Distributors.

projects from a metal panel that closes the fireplace opening. The projecting stove, supported on metal legs, above a noncombustible hearth extension, heats the room like a conventional wood stove, while smoke and combustion gases flow into the panel-sealed fireplace and up the chimney. This type, too, provides easy installation. Also, though it projects into the room, it occupies a minimum of floor space. The two types of in-the-fireplace stoves are shown in figs. 115 and 116.

FIREPLACE STOVES

What you probably think of as a modern free-standing fireplace is technically designated as a fireplace stove. Some of its most familiar forms are shown in figs. 117 and 118. As they vary widely in form and size, you follow the manufacturer's instructions as to wall clearances and floor protection. If the unit is an approved type (which it should be) clearances and floor protection will be based on the results of tests by a recognized testing organization. Typically, the floor protection (in this case called a hearth extension) must extend at least 8″ beyond the stove at the back and sides, and at least 16″ beyond it in the front.

The material requirements, however, are different from those for stoves classed as room heaters. For a fireplace stove, the upper surface of the protective hearth extension should be high enough above the existing floor to prevent floor covering like carpet from being placed on it. For this reason, it's usually made of materials like brick, concrete, stone or tile. In no case may the thickness be less than ⅜″.

Fig. 117. This free-standing fireplace (technically a fireplace stove) is a wood burner with ash drawer for dust-free ash removal. Available in decorator colors, it's shipped pre-assembled, with screens to fit, and telescoping pipe for 8′ ceiling height. It's a Regency model by Majestic. This company also makes the thermo-siphoning chimney required.

Fig. 118. Another fireplace stove design. This is a
Sherwood model by Templet Industries, Inc. It
can be used with insulated Metalbestos factory-
made chimney or other approved type. Triple back
wall of unit permits use within 12″ of combustible
room wall.

INSTALLING A STOVE OR FIREPLACE STOVE

Before you start any installation job, determine exactly where the stove is to be located. This is usually done by placing it temporarily at the approximate location, after measuring for the required clearances. You can then make a trial assembly of the flue connector pipe (stovepipe) from the stove to the chimney opening. If the chimney is walled over, making it necessary for the pipe to pass through the wall surface to reach it, all combustible wallboard and framing must be trimmed away from the connection area to provide at least 18″ clearance, unless an approved protective collar is used to permit reduced clearance.

Horizontal runs of the connector pipe should be as short as possible, never more than 75 percent of the height of the chimney flue above the connection point. The horizontal runs of the pipe should also be pitched upward from the stove to the chimney connection not less than ¼″ per lineal foot. If the pipe connects to an existing masonry chimney, the cross sectional area of the chimney flue should be at least 25 percent greater than that of the pipe in order to assure adequate draft. The diameter of the connector pipe itself should match the diameter of the connecting collar on the stove.

If the connector pipe runs straight up from the stove to a factory-made chimney starting in the ceiling, the starter fitting may automatically provide the necessary clearance to adjacent combustibles by means of protective features in its design. Many starter fittings do. If you don't find information on this in the chimney instructions, check with the manufacturer.

The trial assembly of the connector pipe shows you exactly what pipe trimming, if any, is needed. If trimming is necessary to shorten a length of the pipe, it should be done at the plain (uncrimped) end, using tin snips in most cases. With snips, the easiest method usually consists of cutting inward on a spiral from the end, then around a pencil-marked cut-off line. If the metal of the pipe is too thick for the convenient use of snips, you can use a hacksaw and sabre saw for the trimming. With the hacksaw, make a starting cut long enough to admit a fine-toothed metal cutting sabre saw blade. Then use the sabre saw to cut around the pencil-marked cut-off line. The sabre saw does the job quickly but must be guided evenly while the pipe is held firm on a workbench or work table and rotated as the cut progresses. In many instances, however, trimming can be avoided entirely by shifting the stove a few inches, provided the required clearances are retained.

The connector pipe should enter the chimney flue through a thimble made for the purpose, and available from masonry suppliers. As these thimbles are not always available in the smaller sizes common to wood stove connector pipes, a metal enlarging fitting made for the connector pipe should be used at the chimney entrance. These are sold by hardware stores, and often by wood stove dealers. This arrangement provides a snug fit at the chimney without cement which would make removal of the pipe for cleaning or replacement difficult. Measure to the inside of the chimney with a ruler so your connector pipe can be inserted with its inner end flush with the flue lining. If it extends farther into the flue it will retard the draft.

Once the trial assembly is completed, the floor under the stove location can be prepared. While the stove is still in place, mark the area to be protected. Then move the stove out of the way, and remove any floor covering from the marked area. A straight edge and a single-edged razor or trimming knife can be used to cut the carpet neatly. Save the removed piece if there's any chance you may relocate the stove at a later date. If you plan to use brick or tile on top of the sheet metal over the area, plan your carpet cut-out so that the bricks or tiles will come out even along each side. Even if you use sheet metal alone, it's wise to plan its dimensions this way in case you decide to dress it up later with masonry units, for a change of decor.

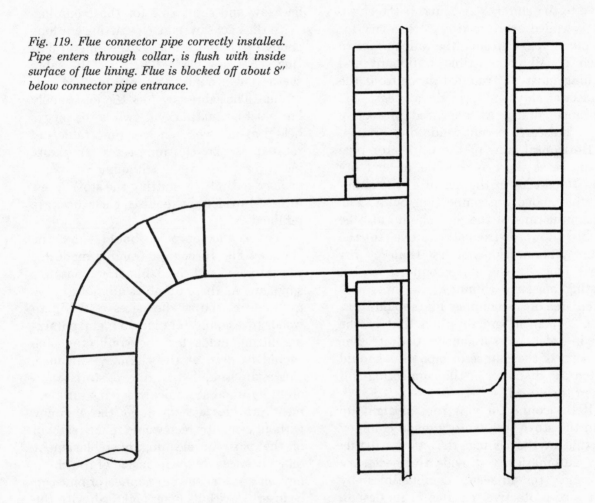

Fig. 119. Flue connector pipe correctly installed. Pipe enters through collar, is flush with inside surface of flue lining. Flue is blocked off about 8" below connector pipe entrance.

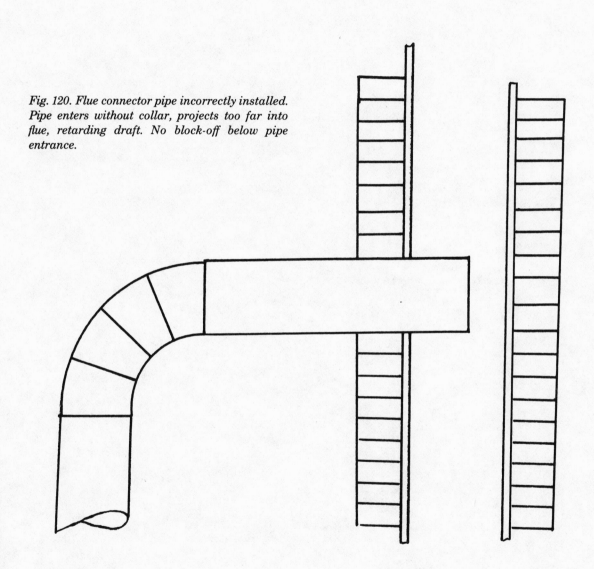

Fig. 120. Flue connector pipe incorrectly installed. Pipe enters without collar, projects too far into flue, retarding draft. No block-off below pipe entrance.

IV
Heating with Style

6

DIFFERENT KINDS OF FIREPLACES, WOOD STOVES AND ACCESSORIES

Choose your fireplace or wood stove the way you would select your furniture or drapes: to suit your taste, to complement the design of your home and to fit the lifestyle of your family. You may even want more than one fireplace or wood stove, or a combination of the two, depending on the size of your home and pocketbook. The factory-made chimneys described in Chapter 4 not only bring down the cost of such installations, but also, in many instances, allow multiple flues to fit. An old type masonry chimney housing more than one flue would be too massive and would require much re-designing in an existing house. If you are planning your installation to be built into a new house, your options are wide open. Let your budget be your guide.

THE TRADITIONAL FIREPLACE . . . FOR CASUAL OR FORMAL ROOMS

The term "traditional," when applied to fireplaces, wears many faces, depending on your own version of what is or is not traditional, and in relation to the style and period of your own home. For example, the traditional fireplace in a Georgian house is very different from the traditional fireplace in a rustic hunting lodge.

An early American style Cape Cod or Saltbox type house is a natural for a fireplace designed to contain a crane for holding a cook-pot or grille and, if room allows, a built-in Dutch oven next to the fireplace proper. As described later, these can prove a boon during a power outage. And collecting old-fashioned cooking equipment at auctions, flea markets and housewreckers is not only fun; one day your collection may be worth a lot of money. However, equipment of this type is also available new from fireplace and specialty shops, and they faithfully follow the original designs and materials, making it possible to furnish your old-style fireplace quickly and easily.

For a fireplace of this type, used brick combined with a heavy old beam in lieu of a mantel will contribute to the authenticity of the design. Used brick is available from the housewrecker's yard, not always in

Fig. 121. Exterior trim on this heat-circulating fireplace by Majestic suits it to a formal room. Intake and outlet grilles are so placed that they do not intrude on the design, but contribute to the efficiency of the fireplace. The firepot on the hearth is a traditional fire starter.

Fig. 122. Kitchen fireplace in 1790 house, Danbury, Conn., with original crane and other facilities for cooking. Fireplace and chimney, built over 185 years ago, are still in use.

Different Kinds of Fireplaces, Wood Stoves and Accessories   131

large quantity, but enough for a fireplace front. This is also the place to look for a big old beam for your mantel or lintel. When you find it, it may be encrusted with dirt, soot or old cement, depending on its original purpose, but don't despair . . . the messier it looks, the cheaper to buy, and the older and mellower its appearance when you refinish it. A word here . . . be careful when cleaning up an old piece not to lose the patina of age. Use a scraper gently to remove real dirt and soil, cement, plaster and such, then wipe with turpentine and allow to dry. Next, try various finishes (on the side that will not show in the final installation) until you get the effect you want.

Another source of large timbers that can be used for such mantels is the sawmill. They can be located in the Yellow Pages of a phone book for outlying areas. Here you can have the beam cut to your specifications, and the marks of the saw add to the old-time style and make it unnecessary to resort to "distressing" the piece, as is too often done in attempts to duplicate old woodwork. After all, the sawmill was the source of most old beams unless you go back to the adze. If your piece is from a sawmill, make sure it is reasonably air-dried before use so that it will not shrink away from its surroundings and fastenings after the fireplace is in use. Material from the wrecker will, of course, be fully seasoned.

Today, many contemporary homes use a version of the early American fireplace and it is completely at ease with this newer type of architecture. Current emphasis on natural materials used to their fullest advantage, and with an eye on using the fireplace not only as a source of heat but as a focal point for congenial family fun and entertaining, has brought about some changes without really altering the basic design. The cooking facilities are more in evidence than in recent years, and the raised hearth, extended as fancy dictates, offers extra seating space. What a welcome spot on a cold wintry night, or after a good day's ice-skating or skiing, not to mention an afternoon's snow removal job, be it by shovel, blower or plow!

In many Colonial homes the fireplace front was plastered, creating a pleasant contrast with dark beams and providing a bright background for the traditional black iron utensils. If this style appeals to you, it eliminates the brickwork that may be tedious for the do-it-yourselfer, as solid concrete block, with an 8 x 16″ face may be used instead of the 4 x 8″ faced brick. After construction, a smooth "buttering" of white cement completes the masonry work.

In many modern homes the fireplace front may be a smooth façade designed to suit the room. It can take many forms. Some are fairly narrow, with the emphasis on height. Here, for instance, it is fitted between large glass areas where the fire is desirable but the view is an integral part of the room's decor. (See fig. 124.) If the fireplace is situated on a north wall, it may be surrounded cozily by bookshelves. If, on the other hand, the fireplace wall is too tall top to bottom, a horizontally extended front can carry the eye outward for a pleasing effect. A raised hearth is also a good decorating ploy here, as all the horizontals tend to minimize unwieldy height. This system also helps when the fireplace wall appears too narrow.

A smooth façade, discreetly colored to contrast or blend with the other colors in the room, can add dramatic impact, according to the effect you desire. Remember that

Fig. 123. Living room fireplace in 1790 house has a smooth plastered surround that contrasts pleasingly with mellow wood tones of mantel and ceiling beams. Like the kitchen fireplace, this one is almost 200 years old and still performs beautifully.

Fig. 124. Slender design of this fireplace allows it to fit in window wall design of contemporary room. Majestic makes it.

Fig. 125. Horizontal styling by Heatilator, with a raised hearth that includes log storage below, adds width to a narrow fireplace wall.

Fig. 126. This raised hearth fireplace offers seating space on cold nights, also houses fire tools like
matched set in stand by Portland Willamette Co.
Mesh-curtain and glass-door screen combination
adds safety to beauty.

Fig. 127. Elegant marble fireplace front with
accessories to suit, in the Savings Bank of Danbury, Conn.

Different Kinds of Fireplaces, Wood Stoves and Accessories   135

light colors tend to make objects appear larger, darker tones to make them shrink. Thus, with color, you can change the over-all effect of your fireplace with the wipe of a brush. Your masonry supplier can advise you about the paint to use.

If your budget is fairly high, your smooth façade may be of marble, slate, metal or other material that takes your fancy. This type may call for professionals for the installation, as special techniques, adhesives and/or fastenings may be required for a good job. Here again, your masonry supplier can guide you to the techniques you'll use if you want to try it yourself, or to the expert your particular job requires.

Fig. 128. This side-opening fireplace by Majestic is enclosed in smooth, easy-to-use paneling and serves as a room divider between the areas it heats.

Another choice for a smooth front is paneling. Available in an extremely wide range of woods and wood-grained materials, paneling is light in weight, easy to work with and blends nicely with most modern day interiors. It is a natural in a paneled playroom but just as compatible in a library or other more formal setting. Since the panels are prefinished, there is little extra work involved in the installation. An assortment of moldings to match, blend or contrast with the wood in the panels makes a neat, professional job a cinch for the amateur who desires a custom look with little outlay. But observe code clearances.

Textured materials, such as different kinds of brick, tile, molded concrete block and hand-textured concrete and plaster are compatible with a modern decor; they also blend happily with simple, more primitive

Fig. 129. Paneling surrounds the in-the-fireplace stove (by the Wilton Stove Works) in a more traditional room. The in-the-fireplace stove greatly increases the efficiency of the original fireplace, while leaving its charm intact.

decorative motifs. The natural color of the material used or color introduced into cement and concrete products help you achieve beautiful results.

If, on the other hand, your taste calls for a more elaborate fireplace front with, for example, paneling, mirrors and a more formal style altogether, it may be cheaper and easier than you think. You can even transform a simple, humdrum fireplace into a charming prototype with very little effort and money. Stock moldings from your local lumberyard, assembled in a pleasing pattern and proportioned to suit your room, can do the trick. However, if you have your heart set on an authentic reproduction of an elegant Adam mantel, it is best to work through an architect or decorator.

When you do not have the time or inclination to do it yourself, ready-made fronts in a wide variety of decorative styles are available at large lumberyards. If these do not fill the bill, one can be made to order at a millwork shop, although this will cost you considerably more. A better bet: a trip to the housewrecker's yard. There you can often find a ready-made front from a mansion of days gone by, that requires only a fresh coat of paint to make it fit your scheme. Or you may find a strip of elaborately carved wood that can be surmounted on an existing front to add distinction to an otherwise dull façade. Here, too, is a source of unusual tiles, old marble, et cetera, at a fraction of the cost of new material. Also, real wood carvings that can be applied singly or in groups to make up a pattern, can be purchased new at cabinetmaker's supply houses like Albert Constantine and Son, Inc. in New York, N.Y.

Fig. 130. Clean lines of simple concrete block fireplace front designed by the Portland Cement Association contrast well with adjacent wall of vertical planking. This is a job that can be executed by most do-it-yourselfers.

Fig. 131. Textured cement lends a touch of primitive charm to this old-time design in a kitchen-dining area. Accessories that really work add to the overall feeling of warmth. A Heatilator unit is the basic fireplace.

Fig. 132. Fireplace mantel assemblies in traditional designs, adjustable so the do-it-yourselfer can reduce both height and width to suit his own fireplace opening, are now available at lumberyards. Constructed of ponderosa pine, they are packaged with instructions that facilitate both professional and do-it-yourself installation. And, of course, the pine lends itself to a wide variety of finishes. National Woodwork Manufacturers Association.

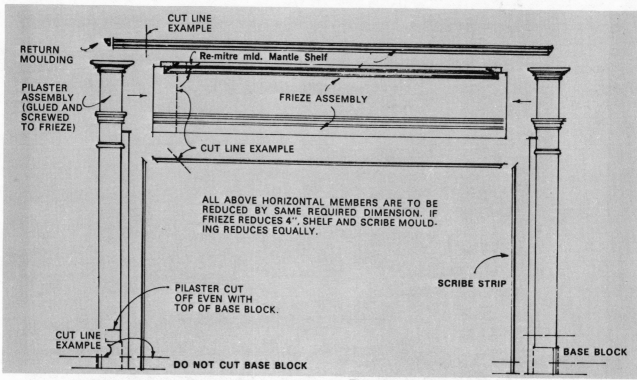

CUT LINE
EXAMPLE

RETURN
MOULDING

PILASTER
ASSEMBLY
(GLUED AND
SCREWED
TO FRIEZE)

Re-mitre mld. Mantle Shelf

FRIEZE ASSEMBLY

CUT LINE EXAMPLE

ALL ABOVE HORIZONTAL MEMBERS ARE TO BE
REDUCED BY SAME REQUIRED DIMENSION. IF
FRIEZE REDUCES 4″, SHELF AND SCRIBE MOULD-
ING REDUCES EQUALLY.

SCRIBE STRIP

PILASTER CUT
OFF EVEN WITH
TOP OF BASE BLOCK.

CUT LINE
EXAMPLE

DO NOT CUT BASE BLOCK

BASE BLOCK

Fig. 133. Drawing shows how members can be saw-cut for reducing height and width in this mantel. National Woodwork Manufacturers Association.

Fig. 134. Formal mantel in another traditional design can also be purchased at your lumberyard. National Woodwork Manufacturers Association.

Fig. 135. A simple Colonial mantel that blends with a paneled wall. National Woodwork Manufacturers Association.

FIREPLACE SCREENS AND OTHER EQUIPMENT

There are many types of firescreens, as shown in figs. 136-140, all designed to keep flying sparks out of your room, a safety measure that should not be ignored. The old folding model must be moved each time you tend the fire, as must the flat type that fits snugly against the fireplace opening. The curtain screen, mounted directly on the fireplace opening and operated much like draw-drapes at a window, is easy to use and requires no storage space. There is a wide price range here, so it pays to shop for the screen that will serve you and your decor at the lowest price.

To support the fire, log rests, firebaskets and andirons offer a choice of styles and designs. Most of the baskets and log rests are high enough to permit the shanks of andirons to slide under them so that the convenience of the former and the decorative beauty of the latter can work together, although any of them can be used singly.

Firebaskets should be chosen with the shape of your fireplace in mind: use a splayed-end basket in the usual splay-sided fireplace, a square-ended model in most contemporary square-sided types. Some firebaskets are convertible, being made with removable ends. With the ends on, the basket can be used as a grate for burning

Fig. 136. Portland Willamette Co. designed this elaborate curtain firescreen, with allowance for andirons (part of the ensemble) and a matched set of tools in a stand.

Fig. 137. Double-frame door screen to fit the fireplace arch is custom-made by Portland Willamette Co. to fit inside or outside the opening.

Fig. 138. This folding glass firescreen by Portland
Willamette Co. is available with a mesh curtain
accessory for further protection when the added
heat from an open fire is desired.

Fig. 139. A Glassfyre screen by Portland
Willamette Co. made to fit a modern two-sided
fireplace. Tools, in their stand, are made by the
same company.

Fig. 140. Firebasket, sometimes called a log grate, can be seen through this Glassfyre screen by Portland Willamette Co. Mesh curtain behind the glass doors is for use when the open fire is used for extra heat.

coal; with the ends removed, logs long enough to reach the sides of the fireplace can be supported on it.

Carriers for coal and wood make for ease in transporting your fuel from its main storage place to the fireside. Of course, the same carriers are also used with wood stoves. Metal log carriers may be elegant brass, or simple black or a combination of the two. Canvas and leather carriers are most practical for actually carrying logs, and some can be opened to fit inside a wood or metal frame, or they can be rolled up and stowed away and the logs placed in the more decorative metal carrier at the hearthside. Coal scuttles can be as simple as plain galvanized steel, wrought iron black or brilliant enameled colors, and decorated in a variety of styles. If price is a prime consideration, choose a plain metal one and paint it to blend with your stove or fireplace.

When there is plenty of room next to your fireplace or wood stove, a log hoop, free-standing and usually of black enameled steel, holds a very large supply. Be sure the logs are not wet with snow or ice when you put them in it, else they will drip onto the floor, with resultant damage and mess.

An excellent solution to the wet log situation is the use of an old-fashioned galvanized laundry tub. Paint the tub inside and out, and decorate the exterior with any motif you like. Sometimes with the use of masking tape it is a simple matter to do the raised ridges in a contrasting color for a striking effect. If you are lucky enough to locate one at an antique dealer's, an old-fashioned copper clothes boiler, polished and gleaming, is truly handsome, but expensive. With this tub storage, when snowy, icy weather catches you with an inadequate supply of wood inside, you can bring in your logs and put them in your tub. In a short time the warmth of the house will dry them sufficiently for use, and the moisture that drains off the logs will soon evaporate. Incidentally, this routine adds a small amount of humidity, often welcome during the heating season.

Fig. 141. Solid brass ensemble by Portland Willamette Co. adds the final touch of elegance combined with safety, convenience and availability of extra logs to this lovely fireplace.

Different Kinds of Fireplaces, Wood Stoves and Accessories 145

TOOLS FOR TENDING THE FIRE

Fireplace tools can be purchased singly or in matched sets. Sets usually come in a stand to place on the hearth, but some folks prefer to simply hang the tools on handsome heavy hooks set in the masonry work around the fireplace itself, or on a metal rack mounted on an adjacent wall. This is a matter of taste, and naturally depends on the type of room the fireplace is in.

The tools consist of tongs, for placing and turning logs, a poker for stirring up a grand blaze, a shovel for putting on coal, if

Fig. 142. Bellows add that extra touch to this set of fireplace tools made to complement the contemporary screen and log basket, all by Portland Willamette Co.

that is your fuel, and for removing ashes in any case. An attractive brush or small broom for hearth clean-up is also handy. Bellows—in many materials and decorated in many ways, from brass ornamentation to simple, handsome leather work—come in a wide price range; they can add to the natural draft when necessary to get the fire started or to revive a waning one. Another old-time accessory is the fire-lighter which is a pretty metal pot, usually of brass or copper, sometimes black iron, with a lid made with a slot to admit a taper or other dipping tool. The pot is filled with kerosene. To use the lighter, pull out the dipping tool, light the wet end, and hold under the paper and kindling in the log rest or basket to start your fire. If you are worried about spills where children and pets play, this is an accessory that can be eliminated or stored out of their reach.

You are in luck if your masonry chimney is equipped with a crane, but if it is not, one can be installed in the existing masonry. (Many Franklin fireplaces on the market today are so equipped.) The crane makes fireplace cooking simple and fun for the whole family. Ready-made grilles are available with hangers to slide onto the crane and are great for broiling meat and chicken, fish or burgers, and can also serve as support for kabobs. Long forks for the traditional marshmallow toasting make for an extra party touch. And what a boon this equipment is when there is a power outage and you have a houseful of hungry people.

When a Dutch oven roaster is suspended from the crane, casseroles and soups, not to forget the good soda bread described in Chapter 1, make for a varied menu. And as you heat and cook with the same equipment and fuel, you save money.

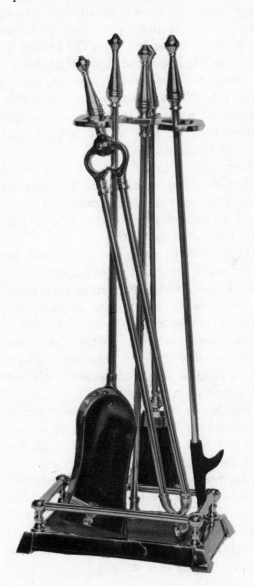

Fig. 143. This tool set comes complete with its own stand and makes using your fireplace simple and practical. From Portland Willamette Co.

WOOD STOVES COME IN MANY FORMS

Today there is a wood stove to suit most homes, old or new, especially when you discover that the popular "free-standing fireplace" is technically considered a "fireplace stove" by manufacturers and testing authorities. The conical type is very versatile as it can be fitted into a corner in a small room, thereby conserving floor space, as well as in the more conventional setting along a wall. In more spacious rooms, one can even be suspended from the ceiling by chains, and it is so constructed that the fire is exposed to view from all sides, as shown in fig. 145. This arrangement offers a dramatic focal point for social occasions, and assures that no one is left out of that welcome circle of heat.

Rectangular models can be adapted to many different types of rooms. In a strictly modern room, the clean lines and functional styling of the stove and flue pipe make their own statement.

The potbelly stove is a natural for family or playrooms. It takes a minimum of space, has a cooktop for fun or emergency use and blends easily into an informal setting. It can be installed almost anywhere in the room, so long as the structural members allow for the chimney's set-up, and its position doesn't interfere with normal activities in the room.

The log or box stove may be a simple unadorned steel firebox on legs, or a truly beautiful and elaborate cast-iron display piece. Since they have cooktops, they serve two purposes, and the more distinctively designed models are not at all out of place in the dining room or the dining area of a country house. One can spread its warmth through a large part of any house, not just the room where it is installed.

Fig. 144. Corner installation of this fireplace stove takes little living space from the room. Designed by Majestic.

The parlor stove, like the one shown in fig. 88 in Chapter 4, was used in times past not only in the parlor but in bedrooms, libraries and any other room where a decorative heater was more practical (as it radiated its heat) than a fireplace. Like the log and box stoves, they were (and are) capable of heating a large area, such as a living-dining room combination, or a bed-dressing-bath suite. These stoves lend themselves easily to many decorative motifs. And you don't have to be hidebound about that either. An antique stove

Fig. 145. Everyone in the room can face the fire's cheery glow with this fireplace stove by Majestic, hung from the ceiling and open on all sides.

Fig. 146. Where space is limited, the potbelly stove is the answer. This model by Portland Stove Foundry, Inc. is handsome too. It serves two purposes, as the cooktop can save the day when icy weather causes a power outage. It renders a tremendous amount of heat for its size.

can readily become the conversation piece in a contemporary room. After all, they are functional in the extreme.

To most of us, the Franklin stove (or fireplace) is the granddaddy of them all, and because of its proven performance over the years, it is accepted in any setting. Modern versions may be more suitable in some backgrounds, but the overall design, classic or contemporary, makes it an all round favorite. Embellishments are many and varied, but as a rule follow early

Fig. 147. Handsome log stove from the Portland Stove Foundry, Inc. is beautifully cast. It not only heats, it has an ample cooktop.

American motifs. Some sport a fender, ideal for toasting toes after a good skate or a walk on a snowy day; others have a simple flat apron extension. Most have cooktops.

For a country kitchen, consider the old-fashioned wood burning range. It combines charm with convenience and is always ready at your service, since it is not dependent on the local power station but rather on your own supply of firewood, which can be gathered in the summer months and stored for use in cold. Use of a wood burning range does not mean that you abandon your modern counterpart; simply that you have another efficient stove that also serves as a source of heat when it is needed. Some of the older models are no longer available new but can still be found in housewrecker's yards. And some enterprising manufacturers are duplicating them when they find artisans to make them.

The strictly modern decor has not been neglected by designers of wood burning stoves. The trim styling and wood-tone finish on the circulating wood burner shown in fig. 152 adapt it to this type of interior. The flue is at the rear, so it is inconspicuous, and it can be used with a masonry or factory-made chimney as long as all clearances are as recommended in Chapter 5.

Imported models, like the French kitchen stove available from Preston Distributing Co., of Lowell, Mass., and the Morsø from Denmark, available through Brookfield Fireside, Inc., Brookfield, Conn., are finding their way into the American market. Since part of the fun of decorating is the seeking out of the unusual but pertinent ingredients that go to make up the composition and total impact of a room, it pays to investigate every source. And never forget that mail order houses like Sears and Montgomery Ward may have just the stove and last little accessory you need to complete your decor.

Fig. 149. A contemporary version of the Franklin fireplace by the Wilton Stove Works is of welded steel. Large throat at base of smoke pipe houses damper.

Fig. 150. Here the doors are shown closed on another Franklin fireplace by the Wilton Stove Works. Of welded steel, this model has angled sides that add strength and provide for expansion and contraction of the metal.

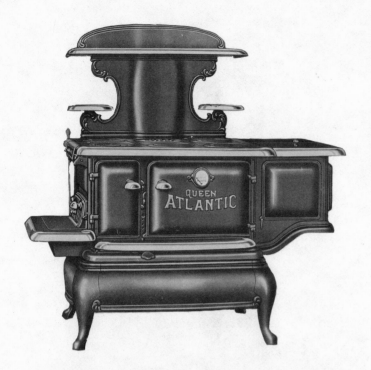

Fig. 151. *This classic design not only heats and cooks, it also serves as a hot water heater. The extension at the right is the hot water reservoir. The copper tank is removable if it is not wanted for any reason, or for repair. This design leaves the entire stovetop clear for culinary use. The oven has removable plates, an oven control damper on top of the range, grates for coal or wood that can be removed from the front. The special satin-black finish requires no "blackening" or polish to keep it bright ... just wipe with a damp cloth. Portland Stove Foundry, Inc.*

Fig. 152. *A wood burning circulator by Ashley Automatic Heater Company is as modern in design as your television set. It is thermostatically controlled for automatic operation.*

V

All About Wood Burning

7

IMPORTANT FACTS—
WHEN YOU PLAN TO
BURN WOOD

There's more than just a warm, cheery glow in a wood fire. A cord of seasoned maple logs packs more heat than a ton of anthracite coal or 200 gallons of residential fuel oil. And some woods, like white oak, are even better than that. So at today's fuel prices, there's gold in that woodpile.

HOW MUCH HEAT IN A LOG?

To appreciate just how much gold, you need only figure your log's heating power the way heating people figure the heating power of fuels like oil and gas—in British thermal units, abbreviated Btu's. A Btu is the amount of heat you need to raise the temperature of one pound of water 1 degree Fahrenheit. In metric terms, this equals 252 calories, or about the heating value of a fried pork chop. To compare the heat in a log pile to the heat in the usual heating fuels you need only rate them all in terms of Btu's. A gallon of No. 2 fuel oil (the kind home-size oil burners use) contains about 140,000 Btu's. A cubic foot of natural gas

contains around 1,000 Btu's, and a pound of well-seasoned sugar maple firewood about 7,677 Btu's. So a 7″ diameter log a little less than 2′ long, weighing around 22 lbs., actually has more heating power than a gallon of oil or 150 cubic feet of gas. Which means that an old-fashioned log fire can do a lot more for you than provide a pleasant atmosphere—in the right kind of fireplace or wood stove it can play a major role in heating your house.

As for efficiency, in general, a wood stove gives you the most usable heat for your money, a circulating fireplace ranks next and a conventional fireplace after that. Today, too, there are many hybrid types, part stove and part fireplace, even stoves that fit in an old-fashioned fireplace and wring a lot more heat out of it than ever before. These were described in detail in parts III and IV. And, of course, there's always the old reliable Franklin stove, mentioned in the previous chapter.

Fig. 153. A good pile of logs like this, some gathered and cut in spring and summer to take advantage of fallen limbs from winter storms, as well as purchased wood, can supply your stove or fireplace over the cold months. Piled on loosely laid patio blocks or gravel to absorb water runoff and prevent rot, they are protected by a sheet of heavy plastic from ice that can lock them together. A few logs atop the plastic anchor it in place. Located in a driveway that is always plowed in winter, the woodpile is always accessible.

HOW TO GET FREE FIREWOOD

Whatever the style of your house-warming wood burner, it can, of course, add a feeling of coziness on a cold night that can't be achieved without it. Whether it can save you money by reducing your heating bills depends not only on its efficiency, but what you pay for firewood. And this can often take on the nature of a game. If you're good at it, the house wins. Usually, you'll have to buy your initial supply, but you can watch the classified ads and shop for a reasonable price.

If you're alert you may hit the jackpot with an occasional, even frequent, load of free firewood. Your chances depend to a considerable extent on your location, sometimes on your ambition. If you live in the suburbs, every dead branch that drops on your lawn is free firewood, and a fallen tree is a bonanza if you have the tools and the determination to cut it up.

If you can borrow a chain saw and you know how to use it, the job won't wear you out. (When you can't borrow the saw you can rent one from a tool rental agency and still have bargain logs.) To cut fallen branches or small trees to log size you can also use the portable circular saw from your workshop, if you're a home handyman. A pair of sawhorses make the job easier. Keep a firm grip on everything, and you can cut first from one side of the branch, then the other, so the cuts meet. This way you can handle larger diameters with a relatively small saw. If you're worried about dulling the blade, buy the throwaway type for this kind of work.

Sometimes, too, your local utility company can be a source of free firewood, and it's always a pleasure to get something for nothing from a utility company! If you see one of their crews cutting up a tree, or part of a tree, to protect the power lines from possible storm damage, ask about the wood. If it's in the giveaway category you may have to take it in greater lengths than you can use without further cutting. But think in terms of that borrowed or rented chain saw.

Another free-wood possibility is sometimes found in lumberyards that have facilities for power-sawing standard lumber sizes to suit customers' needs. This often results in a pile of scrap pieces that make good kindling or stove fuel. And the scrapwood may be yours for the asking. Try it. You may win, and you can't lose. Learn to think firewood, And don't forget your own workshop scraps and burnable trash.

Newspapers also make worthwhile fuel for your wood burner. One of the simplest ways to turn them into heat is simply to roll them into paper logs about 4-5" in diameter and hold them in this shape with a few strips of the cheapest masking tape you can buy. A hole down the center of the roll about as round as your thumb helps them burn. There are other methods that include wetting and drying the paper, and you can buy little rolling tools to do the job. If you're not satisfied with the performance of your easy-way paper logs you can always try the other ways.

FIREWOOD TERMINOLOGY

When you do your firewood shopping you'll usually be dealing in terms of "cords" of wood. The standard cord is a pile 4' wide, 4' high and 8' long. This multiplies out to 128 cubic feet. But since logs are irregular in form and diameter, it's generally assumed that only about 70 percent of a cord-size pile is actually wood. So you really get about 90 cubic feet, which is the figure to use if you do any pound-for-pound Btu figuring, as described earlier.

Another term you may encounter is the "cord run," sometimes also called a cord. This, however, is a pile 4' high and 8' long, but as wide as the length of the logs. It's not used as often as the standard cord, but worth knowing to avoid mixups.

If you have a wood stove you'll probably be buying shorter wood than you would for a fireplace. In 16" lengths, it's often called stove wood, as typical log stoves can take this length. (You may also hear terms like block wood and chunk wood applied to these short pieces.) Don't be misled by the term "cordwood," however, as it often refers to 4' lengths, which aren't likely to fit today's fireplaces. But if you have a suitable saw you can cut a 4' log into two 2-footers or three 16-inchers.

The terminology is likely to vary with the location, as much of it is colloquial. Whatever the terms, be sure you know what you're getting, and that the wood you buy will fit your stove or fireplace. The diameter of the short logs to be used in a wood stove is important too, as they must fit through the fueling door. (A fireplace can handle a wider range of log diameters.) If you're ordering wood, of course you can specify the size you want, but be sure to confirm the overall price, as smaller sizes may have a different price.

FIREWOOD SPECIES AND CREOSOTE

Although householders could once be particular about the exact species of their firewood, the picture has changed. Today, many of the favored firewood species are scarce, some entirely unavailable. And in firewood bargain hunting, you'll often have to take what you can get. In any event, you can be sure there's plenty of potential heat in it, as a cord of the readily available woods (when seasoned) is equal to at least a ton of coal, and a cord of even the poorest firewood species rates close to three-quarters of a ton of coal. But there's more to it than that.

If you have to take green wood, it's wise to let it season well in a dry place if possible before you use it. (If you're ambitious enough to split it with an axe or sledge and wedge, it seasons faster.) If you're ordering it you may be able to order it already split.

One reason for seasoning firewood is, of course, to improve its heating value. There's another good reason, however. Green wood and pitchy wood have a tendency to create a deposit on the inside of the chimney that's often called "creosote" although its chemical formula is a little different. And this is most likely to occur when the wood is burned slowly (as in holding a fire overnight) and when the chimney is exposed to a very cold outside atmosphere. So it's more likely in very cold climates than in mild ones. Green wood may contain as much as 40 percent water compared to 15 or 20 percent in seasoned wood. When it burns slowly it gives off acetic acid and pyroligneous acid which, combined with the water, form the creosote deposit inside the chimney. When the chimney is cold, as on a very frigid night, the vapor condenses on its inside surfaces faster and the deposit builds up more quickly. If the fire is hot and active, however, much of the creosote is carried off into the atmosphere. And, of course, the chimney itself warms up. As might be expected, creosote formation is not as likely in chimneys surrounded by warm rooms.

The problem with creosote is that it can build up to considerable depth over a period of time, and then, when exposed to a hot fire, suddenly ignite inside the chimney. The result can be an internal chimney fire so hot it can seriously damage the chimney and possibly heat the surrounding structure enough to start a house fire. So chimney creosote and its causes are to be avoided. As a precaution, some old timers made it a practice to have a hot, lively fire for at least a brief period each day to burn off any deposit that might be present.

IF YOU CAN CHOOSE YOUR FIREWOOD SPECIES

Although in many areas you may not have much choice, it helps to know the merits of the traditionally favored firewoods, in case you can get them. Oak and ash (the species—not ashes) are usually at the head of the list. Beech is another. Hickory and apple also burn well and give off a pleasant aroma. While you'll often see white birch logs stacked in a fireplace in summer, they're usually for decoration. You can burn them, of course, but birch is a fast-burning species, good for quick rather than prolonged heat. Pine and other evergreen species also burn faster than most hardwoods—one reason they make good kindling.

Many log fire devotees favor a species mixture when they can get it, such as half cedar and half oak. In starting their fires, the cedar lights quickly and provides quick warmth plus ample flame to get the oak burning, after which the oak provides the long-burning fire. One point to remember in regard to firewood is that it's a subject over which you can almost always get into an argument. So if somebody insists there's only one kind of wood fit to burn in your fireplace or wood stove, agree with him. It's probably not available anyway.

HOW TO STORE FIREWOOD

The important points in firewood storage are dryness and convenience. As you'll probably have to store most of your wood out of doors, don't stack it too far from the house. Remember—you may have to collect some off the pile on a cold, snowy night. To keep your outdoor wood (unless you're fortunate enough to have an old-fashioned woodshed) you can use concrete patio blocks as a base for the pile. These are inexpensive and easy to lay. And they keep the bottom layer of logs from rotting from contact with the moist earth.

The simplest and cheapest way to keep the upper part of the pile relatively dry is with a covering of polyethylene sheeting, sold in lumberyards. To keep it from blowing away, weight it down here and there with a small log. When you need a new supply, lift off a weighting log and take what you need, then replace the weight.

Always try to keep a reasonable supply of firewood inside the house to avoid those cold night jaunts to the woodpile. The usual metal log carrier that stands by the hearth holds only enough for a single evening's fire in most cases. A sizable wood box in the basement can replenish it quite a few times. If you have to keep your extra supply where it shows, a big galvanized washtub from the hardware store makes a durable bin. To make it attractive, paint it and decorate it. The tub in fig. 88, Chapter 4 is painted white and embellished with flower patterns based on a Pennsylvania Dutch motif. If you're in a hurry, paint the tub flat black to look like cast iron, and rim the top with gold paint.

To transport your logs from the outdoor pile, a canvas or leather log carrier is your best bet. You can buy one most any place where you can buy other fireplace accessories. A final tip: when your wood supply is delivered (if you buy it) check it over for the assorted insects that may be living in it. If they're present, spray your woodpile with a suitable insecticide before they have a chance to become your household guests. It's wise, too, under these conditions to take an occasional look at your indoor supply.

ABOUT THERMOSTATS

To avoid problems when you use a wood fire for auxiliary heating, it helps to know some of the workings of your regular heating system. It might otherwise respond in mysterious ways to your wood burner's output. For example, some houses with zoned heating systems have several thermostats; others have a single one. Either way, each thermostat responds to the temperature of the room in which it is located. If that room is warmer than the thermostat setting, the thermostat won't turn on the heat for that room. This, of course, means that you'll burn less fuel in your central heating system while the room is being heated by a hearty wood fire.

But in some homes it can also create peculiar situations unless you know what to expect and what to do about it. If, for example, your house has only one thermostat and it happens to be located in the room where the lovely old log stove is generously dispensing its warmth, the thermostat will shut off the heat all over the house. On a cold night this can mean you'll eventually get complaints from the kids upstairs, and later you'll retire to a chilly bed yourself. In some houses you can avoid or at least minimize this problem by leaving a clear path for the heat to reach the other rooms by leaving their doors open. If your wood burner isn't in the same room with the single thermostat the problem isn't as likely to be noticeable. The same is true of multiple thermostat zone heating systems and electrically heated houses with a thermostat in each room.

If you use your log fire only in the evening, as is often the case with a fireplace, the automatic heating system will come on later as the fire dies down. If, however, you have a good supply of cheap firewood and your goal is to keep a wood stove going steadily to reduce your overall heating bill, ask your heating man about possible locations for the thermostat other than in the room with the wood burner. And remember that the radiators or hot air registers in the wood-heated room should be adjusted accordingly. All in all, problems of this type aren't too common. But it pays to know about the possibility, just in case.

Also there are plenty of ways a wood burner can reduce your overall heating bills without burning continuously. If you turn down your thermostat at night, for example, an early riser in the family can light a paper log fire in the wood stove in the morning, and your regular heating system will have less time to run to reach daytime temperature. (If fire-lighting seems like too much of a morning chore, you'll find quick and easy ways of doing it in Chapter 2.) The wood burner can also do an economical and even more welcome job of making things cozy quickly when you return from a few days' trip during which you left the heat turned low. The trick in this type of performance is, of course, that the wood stove operates in addition to the regular heating system during the warm-up period, often doubling the total heat output and bringing the house temperature to the comfort level in a proportionately shorter time.

Last but not least among the economic factors is your personal knack for getting the most out of a wood fire, whether in a wood stove or a fireplace. This comes quickly to most of us. Possibly we have an instinct for it, as our ancestors warmed themselves by wood fires since prehistoric times. Part of the knack lies in recognizing that wood stoves have distinct personalities, according to make and model. Like some cars that can be started in cold weather only by their owners (who know the trick that applies), each stove responds to its own requirements. The reasons behind this are covered in Chapter 2, and they make wood burning more interesting. Fireplaces, too, have their individual traits, though they're usually not as distinct as those of the stoves. But you'll do well to keep them in mind. Sometimes a simple trick can turn a smoky troublemaker into a clean and cozy housewarmer, as detailed in Chapter 8.

FUELS OTHER THAN WOOD

Manufactured logs, fuel briquets, cannel coal, anthracite (hard) coal and some bituminous coals can all be used as well as logs. Some folks prefer coal, especially cannel coal. The manufactured logs are usually available at supermarkets and discount houses in areas where fireplaces and wood stoves are in general use, and they can be purchased singly or by the case. Some brands burn with a brilliantly colored flame; most will hold a fire for an evening.

As to the availability of the various types of coal, that depends on the area where you live. The best way to locate a source is through the Yellow Pages of your phone book. If that doesn't list any, try adjoining towns. In some cases it may be worthwhile to go some distance to pick up a small load. Take suitable containers with you to protect the family car, if that is how you will have to transport it. Some outlets even have some types pre-packaged for this purpose.

Cannel coal, for *fireplaces only,* should *always* be used with an adequate firescreen as its nature is to produce a very hot fire and to send out large sparks in all directions. Sparks of this nature landing on rugs or floors can be dangerous. Anthracite coal, commonly called hard coal, can be used in a fireplace if a suitable grate is provided for its use. (This also applies to bituminous coal.) These are sometimes available from mail order houses, hardware stores and other outlets for fireplace accessories. It can be used in some stoves, if grates are made for the model you have. Follow the manufacturers instructions. In a pinch, say a power failure or great delay in receiving your regular fuel supply, charcoal can do a cooking-and-heating job in your fireplace (*not* without damage risk in a wood stove), but its price makes it impractical for general use in heating.

8

TROUBLE-SHOOTING

Of all the ills the fireplace is heir to, spilling smoke into the room is probably the most annoying and, sometimes, puzzling. But if you know what to look for you can usually find the cause—and the cure. For there's more science than art in fireplace construction and none of the strange magic sometimes attributed to it. There's no mystery, for example, in the fact that some fireplaces smoke and others don't. There isn't even any mystery in the fact that some fireplaces smoke when there's no fire in them—not even cold ashes. More about this shortly.

Wood stoves, too, may occasionally perform in seemingly odd ways, until you know the reasons and the remedies. Then you can often end the trouble in a minute or so with no tools at all and very little work. Most of the time (but not always) there's an answer that won't tax your budget or your handyman's ability. A few basic rules of the burning process (that you probably already know) are your best guide.

We don't have to be told, for example, that hot air rises. If you take a cubic foot of air at 70 degrees from your living room and heat it to 600 degrees (a common chimney temperature) it expands to *two* cubic feet, but it still weighs the same. So, for its "size" it's only half the weight of the unheated air. Because of this heat-produced buoyancy, it rises from the fire in your fireplace and normally floats up the chimney, carrying the smoke with it. But sometimes, instead of floating up the chimney, it floats into the room and up to the ceiling, along with the smoke. The reasons, often surprising, range from advances in home construction to the weather, the birds and just plain blunders.

SIMPLE CAUSES OF FIREPLACE TROUBLE—INCLUDING YOU

To track down smoke trouble always look first for the obvious. Be sure the damper is open. It's easy enough to forget to open it. (It's wise, however, to keep it shut to prevent heat losses up the chimney when the fireplace isn't in use.) Or, if the fireplace is new and you're not accustomed

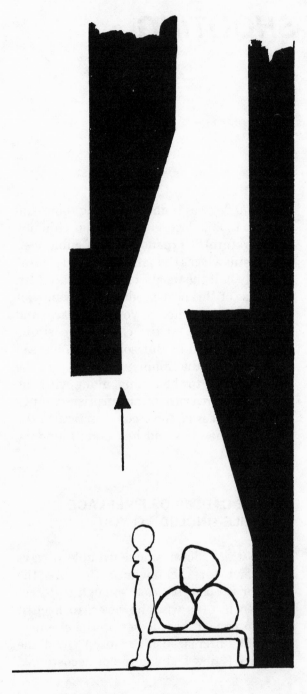

Fig. 154. Don't build your fire farther forward than the inside of the fireplace breast (arrow) or you may get smoke puffs into the room.

to it, you may not be using the damper control properly. Damper controls vary from simple handles to levers you work with a poker. If you've just moved into the house, or have just added a fireplace, acquaint yourself with the workings of the damper before you light your first fire.

Another cause of smoke in the personal error category is in the location of the fire in the hearth. You may have built the fire too far forward, although it may not look that way. This is most likely to happen in a fireplace with a facing of masonry that's thicker than usual, like fieldstone. As the actual opening to the chimney may then be a considerable distance back from the front surface of this facing, your fire can appear to be completely inside the fireplace even when a sizable portion of it is well in front of the chimney opening. So not all of the smoke finds its way back to the chimney and the rest drifts into the room. To prevent this kind of trouble just don't build your fire farther forward than the *inside* of the upper facing of the fireplace. It's best, of course, to check on this before you light the fire, assuming you haven't used the fireplace before. But if smoke is already spilling into the room, and you think this might be the cause, you can usually move the fire back far enough with your tongs and poker.

LOOK BEFORE YOU LIGHT

You can avoid other potential fireplace troubles too by doing a little inspection job before you light your first fire each season. (Or before the first fire in a fireplace you haven't used before.) Assuming the damper has been closed during the summer, open it. Usually at this point nothing happens. But on occasion, anything from birds' nests to squirrels or raccoons may drop into your fireplace. If there's any evidence that uninvited guests have been living in the chimney, look for nests they may have left behind. These can block the flue and cause trouble. (An entire family of raccoons set up summer housekeeping in a chimney without a spark arrester. The arrester, in fact, was installed later as much to keep raccoons out as to keep sparks in.)

To check the flue for obstructions, put on some old clothes and slide far enough into the fireplace to take an upward look with a flashlight. Wear glasses so soot particles won't get in your eyes. (It may take a minute or two for your eyes to adjust to the blackness.) This procedure is especially advisable if you've just moved into the house, particularly if it's an older one. First, it gives you a clear look at the damper and its control, so you'll know how to work it. And secondly, in an aging chimney it may reveal such things as fallen bricks lodged in the flue. If so, get the repairs done before you use the fireplace, as fallen masonry in an old chimney may have left danger points through which sparks could pass. Unless you're skilled at this sort of fix-it work, your best bet is professional help.

If the flue runs straight up from the fireplace to the chimney top and it is unobstructed, you should be able to see daylight at the upper end. If so, you'll know that a quick look up the flue before the start of future heating seasons will show any obstructions, or let you relax with the assurance that all's clear.

THE PERFECT FIREPLACE THAT DOESN'T WORK

Strange as it may seem, top quality home construction can sometimes be responsible for a smoky fireplace. But fortunately the cure is quick and easy, once you recognize the nature of the trouble. You might encounter this type of puzzler in a new, well-built, well-insulated and thoroughly caulked and weather-stripped small home. We'll assume that the fireplace and chimney are properly designed and built. Yet smoke spills into the room whenever the fire is going. The problem here is likely to be what might be called a super-sealed building.

Modern homes, built with panel type sheathing and completely caulked and weather-stripped are sometimes so well sealed that sufficient air for combustion and replacement of chimney outflow simply can't get into the house. (This isn't a problem in most older homes, as enough air seeps in through the house structure.)

In some instances, the fireplace performs perfectly until the basement oil burner switches on, then the fireplace smokes. In this case there's enough replacement air for the fireplace but not for both fireplace and oil burner. So the stronger chimney outflow from the blower-assisted oil burner pulls replacement air from the rest of the house by literally sucking it *down* the fireplace chimney—and the fireplace smokes. But, as explained shortly, you can usually cure the trouble in a matter of seconds.

SMOKE FROM A FIRELESS FIREPLACE

A variation of the tight house problem sometimes occurs when two fireplaces have their flues in the same chimney, ordinarily a perfectly sound practice when fireplaces are located in adjacent rooms. In a super-sealed house, however, if one fireplace is in use and the other is not, the operating fireplace may draw its replacement air down the flue of the unused fireplace along with smoke from the flue of the operating fireplace. This presents the strange phenomenon of an empty fireplace that smokes and a fully fired one that doesn't. The cure for super-sealed house problems of this type takes about half a minute, no tools and almost no effort. Just open a window slightly—in the basement if there's a reasonably free air passage from there to the fireplace area. Then both oil burner and fireplace will benefit. The same measures, of course, apply to central heating burning gas or other fuel.

The problem of smoke or fumes "pouring" from one flue into another can also occur under some conditions in houses that are not tightly sealed. Sometimes it results from wind currents created by roof contours, or nearby trees. If it occurs at all, it's wise to use some means of separating the tops of the flues. The simplest method consists of adding about 6" to the height of one of them. If the chimney is capped, it may be simpler to add partitions between flues. Either measure usually cures the trouble if ample replacement air is also provided in the house.

Fig. 155. If you have a problem with one fireplace flue pulling in smoke from an adjacent flue, or with a fireplace that smokes without a fire in it, add 6" or more to the height of one flue, like this. If in doubt, add more. Flue separation usually cures the trouble.

In some instances, smoke or furnace fumes may issue from a cold fireplace even though the tops of adjacent flues are already separated from each other. In this event you can suspect leakage somewhere inside the chimney from one flue to the other. This can occur where flue tiles of adjacent flues have been placed next to each other uncemented and without brickwork between them. If the tile joints of the adjacent flues are side by side, rather than staggered as they should be, the chance of this kind of trouble is even greater. The cure for this is a job for the professional. In the past it consisted of tearing out the chimney and rebuilding it with the flues properly joined. Today, it's often possible (and more economical) to close off one of the flues and substitute a factory-made metal chimney for it. (See Chapter 4.)

One other old-house fireplace problem results from outside air leaking into the flue through brickwork that has lost its mortar. The colder air from the outside then reduces the temperature of the flue gases on their way up the chimney, often slowing them enough to cause smoking from the fireplace. The cure lies in pointing up the brickwork with new mortar. Unless you're an able hand at this sort of thing and enjoy working on a high ladder, you'll be wise to hire a professional for the job. An important point: when you hire someone for work that involves possible hazards, be sure he is fully insured for the type of work. Your own liability insurance may not cover accidents to people doing work on your house.

In very cold climates some homeowners solve the replacement air problem by replacing a basement window pane with a device called a draft regulator. This has a balanced flap that can be adjusted to open only when the air pressure inside the house is less than the pressure outside, as when the outflow from chimneys calls for replacement air. At all other times the flap remains closed so cold air doesn't enter. The outside end of the regulator can be protected from rain and snow by a down-turned stovepipe elbow. If this interests you, and you're not familiar with such things, ask your heating service man about installing it. He'll be familiar with the draft regulator, as it is ordinarily used in the smoke pipe between a basement furnace and the chimney to control the draft and reduce heat losses up the chimney.

A final tip: if your house is so well sealed it doesn't let in enough air for your fireplace, you'll be wise to add a little ventilation for the benefit of the people, too. So a slightly opened window may be a good idea regardless of other measures.

Fig. 156. An automatic draft regulator, installed in place of one pane of a cellar window, can provide combustion air automatically when your oil burner starts and is often the answer to a fireplace that smokes when the oil burner starts. Use a regulator considerably larger than the one in your oil burner flue connector pipe. It closes when combustion air isn't needed.

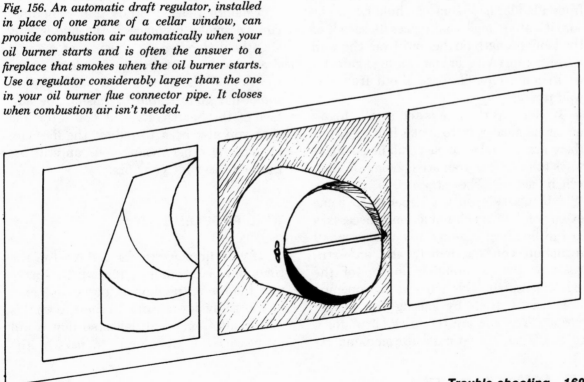

THE FIREPLACE THAT "WAS NEVER RIGHT"

If you buy an older home and later hear that your smoky fireplace "was never right" there's a good chance that the flue is too small for the size of the fireplace. (There can be other troubles but this is the common one.) And there are simple cures.

For a fireplace to perform properly its flue should not have a cross sectional area less than $\frac{1}{12}$ the area of the fireplace opening. If, for example, your fireplace opening adds up to 12 square feet, the inside area of the flue should not be less than 1 square foot. As it's usually not practical to measure the flue size from the fireplace, you may have to measure it from the roof. If so, be careful. If you must climb the roof, fasten a safety rope around yourself and lead it over the peak to a firm anchorage on the other side, so you can't fall over the edge if you slip. If you work from a ladder have someone hold it, and be sure it's at an angle that places its base $\frac{1}{4}$ of the ladder-length farther out from the wall than its top. (A 12′ ladder leaning against a wall should have its base 3′ out from the wall.)

If you find the flue is too small there's no economical way to make it bigger, but there are a number of easy and inexpensive ways to make the fireplace opening smaller, which accomplishes the same purpose. Which method you use depends to some extent on how much reduction is necessary in the fireplace opening area. For a small reduction you can simply add an extra layer or two of firebrick on top of the existing hearth. This narrows the opening from the bottom by raising the hearth surface. You can lay the brick "dry" for a tryout. Then, if that cures the smoking, re-lay the bricks with fireclay sold by masonry suppliers. You can also add a layer of firebrick to each side of the fireplace to reduce the opening width.

Another method very often used calls for a metal hood (frequently just a flat strip of black iron) mounted across the top of the fireplace opening to reduce the area from the top downward. The metal must, of course, be attached to the masonry with suitable masonry fasteners, not to any wooden parts of the mantel. This metal hood also helps if part of the smoking trouble stems from a damper that is set too low (another fault sometimes found in old houses). You can buy the metal from an iron working shop. The shop will also have facilities for punching holes for the masonry fasteners, saving you the work of drilling them with a power drill. You can use your power drill, however, with a masonry bit to drill the right-size holes in the masonry to receive the fasteners.

One other easy method that sometimes cures a smoky fireplace, if the flue is only slightly undersized, is the use of an iron firebasket to contain the fire. This raises the fire off the hearth and has an effect somewhat comparable to raising the surface of the hearth. Even if you later find that you also need to reduce the fireplace opening by other means you can still use the firebasket for your fire.

WIND PROBLEMS

If your fireplace works well most of the time, but occasionally puffs a little smoke into the room, the momentary smoke may be caused by downdrafts. In some cases this can result from wind deflected downward by nearby tall trees or by a part of the

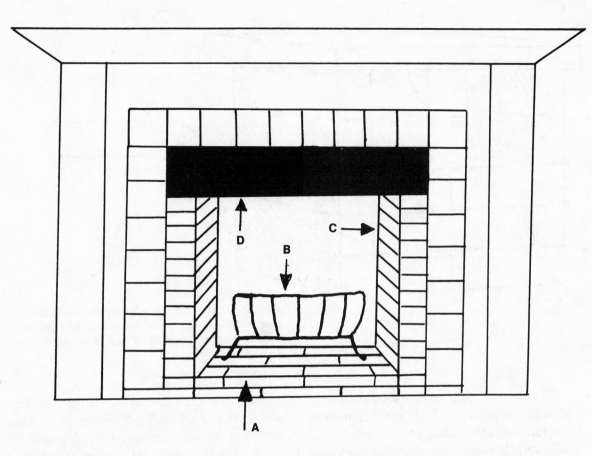

Fig. 157. When the fireplace flue is undersized, you can usually solve the smoke problem by one of several methods, or a combination of them. The object is to reduce the size of the fireplace opening enough to match the flue size. (A) Lay an extra layer of firebrick on the existing firebrick base. This may be all you need. (B) If it isn't enough, *try a fire basket. This raises the fire, has the effect of reducing the fireplace opening size. (C) If you need more size reduction, add a course of firebrick up each side of the fireplace. (D) If you need still more opening size reduction, use a sheet iron hood across the top of the fireplace opening, sized to make the size reduction.*

house roof. In general, short chimneys are more likely to be affected than tall ones, as the updraft in a tall chimney is usually greater than in a short one.

The remedy depends on the situation. If the top of the chimney is obviously below a roof contour that deflects wind down the chimney, consider increasing the chimney height. This can often be done quickly and economically with a double-walled insul-ated metal extension with a cross section equal to that of the flue. Fittings are available, as shown in Chapter 4, to mount this type of chimney on existing masonry. And, of course, masonry may be used to extend the chimney and increase the height without altering the original style. Whether you try it yourself or hire a professional depends on your skill, your free time and your ambition.

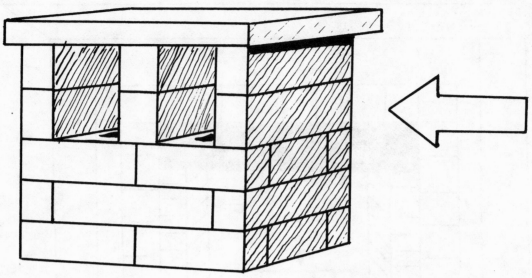

Fig. 158. If the prevailing wind (arrow) is deflected downward by roof contours or nearby trees or hills, cap the chimney like this and partition the flues to block the wind.

Where very tall trees (sometimes on adjacent property) or high ground nearby (like an abruptly rising hill) produce the downdraft, it may not be feasible to extend the chimney enough to effect a remedy. Adding a hooded top to the chimney, however, usually does the trick, as the downdraft comes from a single direction in such cases. Simply build the chimney hood so its walls block the wind from that direction.

In rare instances you may find a chimney built without a smoke shelf, which makes it considerably more likely to puff smoke into the room from downdrafts. It's seldom practical to add a smoke shelf, but a little extra height or a hooded top may help somewhat.

One simple chimney feature that has long been accepted as a help to the smooth flow of smoke is the beveled top which tends to deflect wind upward. It also as-

sures quick drainage of rain from the masonry. If the offending chimney lacks this, it's easy to add, though a hood would be more effective and has the advantage of keeping rain out of the flue. This eliminates the possibility of a sooty trickle from the hearth during a prolonged rainy spell in summer.

SPARK ARRESTERS AND SQUIRREL STOPPERS

Spark arresters are seldom required under average conditions. But if your fireplace or wood stove chimney is in a forested area, near a combustible roof or some other fire hazard, it's wise to equip it with one. Typically, it's made of wire mesh (available at hardware stores), though some are made of expanded or perforated metal.

For residential use on a capped masonry chimney, they should have vertical sides that extend upward at least 9″, with a gross surface area at least twice the cross sectional area of the flue. (For pre-fab metal chimneys, follow the manufacturer's recommendations.) The arrester material should be mounted outside the flue area and thoroughly anchored to the chimney top. Welded mesh is preferable.

Wire mesh openings shouldn't be larger than ⅝″ nor smaller than ⁵⁄₁₆″. While the spark arrester can't completely eliminate all spark discharge, it blocks the larger particles that are most likely to cause trouble. And it protects your chimney from uninvited guests like nesting birds, squirrels and raccoons. If you make your own, plan it for easy removal and replacement, as you'll eventually need a new one. To play safe, if you need a spark arrester, take a close look at it at least at the beginning and end of the heating season, more often if its condition is questionable.

WOOD-STOVE PROBLEMS

As most wood stoves, especially the traditional types, have had ample testing, stove troubles are usually more likely to stem from installation or operation errors than from the stove design. Chimney troubles, of course, can affect a wood stove's performance in much the same way that they affect a fireplace. But since most chimney flues are larger than the usual wood stove smoke pipe, you're not likely to face an undersized flue problem. Wood stoves, on the other hand, sometimes have their own chimney problems that seldom affect fireplaces.

POOR DRAFT

If a wood stove smokes, check the obvious things first, as with a fireplace, starting by making sure the damper is open. Then look for the type of chimney troubles that are peculiar to the wood stove. If the smoke pipe from the stove is connected into an existing masonry chimney that was formerly used for a fireplace or other heating unit, make certain that all openings into the flue, other than the stovepipe opening, are thoroughly sealed. If the stovepipe enters the flue above a fireplace previously served by the flue, the fireplace damper should be closed and made airtight.

If, instead of a fireplace, a central heating unit in the basement was originally connected to the flue, you can close the old connection hole with brick and cement mortar. If such openings are not tightly sealed they can admit cold air that can cause sluggish draft and possible fire hazards. (Unused chimney flues and walled-over fireplaces are most often found in older homes that have had some remodeling and sometimes a new heating system. For safety, check the condition of the chimney before reactivating the unused flue.) Unless the portion of the flue below the stove connection is to be used at a later date, you can block it off, leaving a "soot pocket" about 8″ deep below the connection. This prevents the usual season's soot accumulation from obstructing the end of the smoke pipe, but it doesn't permit an excessive accumulation of soot, which can catch fire under some conditions and create a hazard. The soot pocket can be vacuumed out if necessary, by removing the smoke pipe temporarily. (One method sometimes used to block off the lower portion of the flue begins by wedging a layer of wire mesh into it below the smokepipe opening, by reaching in through the opening. Cement is then spread on top of the mesh and allowed to set, forming the base of the soot pocket.)

Sluggish or smoky stove performance can also result from a smoke pipe that extends too far into the chimney. The open end of the pipe is then blocked by the opposite side of the flue. To check this (if you didn't check during the installation), remove the smoke pipe from the chimney (when the stove is cold) and use a yardstick to measure the distance through the chimney to the other side of the flue. At the same time measure the thickness of the chimney masonry to the inside of the flue at the entry point of the smoke pipe. The pipe should not extend into the chimney more than the thickness of this masonry. Mark the pipe accordingly, and trim off any excess length with metal snips.

When you replace the pipe it should fit snugly into the entrance hole. If it doesn't, fill in any gaps with cement or fire clay. A loose fit admits cool air that slows the draft. Under some conditions it can also allow the passage of live sparks.

CREOSOTE

If the fire in the stove is frequently "held" overnight as a slow, smoldering fire, it's a good idea to check the inside of the smoke pipe at frequent intervals (when the fire is out and the stove cold) and after any significant sign of smoky operation that didn't occur before. When wood is burned slowly, it gives off chemicals that combine to form "creosote," as described in Chapter 7. This condenses on the inside of the flue, especially in very cold weather when the chimney walls are chilled. In tests, creosote has sometimes built up to a thickness of more than an inch, which is enough to cause sluggish, sometimes smoky, operation. But much more important, it can ignite and cause a dangerous internal chimney fire. To minimize the chance of creosote accumulation, follow the precautions outlined in Chapter 7.

DON'T STRANGLE YOUR FIRE

In general, it's wise not to aim for the slowest possible fire when you want your wood stove to keep a room cozy overnight. A little flame above the firewood reduces the creosote problem and lessens the chance of killing the draft, a possibility on a very cold night. Without sufficient heat flow from the stove, an outside chimney can actually chill through and further slow the weak draft. This, in turn, reduces the heat passing up the chimney still more until the draft is barely detectable. If the stove room happens to be one that's normally on the cold side when the stove isn't operating, still more of the heat will be dissipated into the room, until the draft is so close to zero that smoke begins to find its way through minor gaps in the stove shell. By morning, this can result in a smoke-filled room definitely disconcerting to early risers and even more disconcerting to the housekeeper of the family, to say nothing of the pervading chill, rather than welcoming warmth. To avoid this, make your overnight fire-holding tests a trifle on the high side rather than the low side until you get the knack. The chilled-chimney, smoky-room situation isn't too common, but if you know what can cause it, you'll probably never have to worry about it.

Appendices

APPENDIX I

*HOW TO HOLD ON
TO THE HEAT*

If you've turned to wood burning to help cut your regular heating bills, you also want to hold on to as much heat as possible. To determine what insulation can do for you, you need only some basic figures and a little simple arithmetic.

HOW MUCH HEAT ARE YOU LOSING?

The insulating ability of practically all home construction and insulating materials has already been determined by tests. These tests actually showed how many British thermal units (heat measuring units described in Chapter 7) leak through a square foot of the material, 1″ thick, in an hour if the temperature on one side is 1 degree F. higher than the temperature on the other side. The amount of heat that leaks through is called the "K value." Fiberglass, for example, has a K value of about .27, which means that a little more than ¼ of a Btu leaks through a 1″ thick square foot of it in an hour, with a 1 degree inside-outside temperature difference. From

there on you simply multiply. If the temperature difference is 5 degrees you multiply .27 by 5 and find you're losing 1.35 Btu's each hour. If you're figuring on the basis of 1,000 square feet at the 5 degree difference, you multiply again by 1,000 and find that your overall heat loss is 1,350 Btu's (1.35 x 1,000). At this point you can begin to tie your heat loss to dollars and cents. If you heat with gas, for example, a cubic foot of it provides about 1,000 Btu's and you're losing more than that through the 1,000 square foot sample, each hour.

When the heat loss per square foot per hour is based on the thickness of the product being used, instead of 1″ thickness, it's called the "C value." The C value of gypsum board, for example, is about 2.25, which means 2.25 Btu's will pass through it each hour at a 1 degree temperature difference. So the K and C values tell you how much heat you lose through the different materials of different thicknesses. But you need to know how well these materials can *block* the loss of heat. And that's told by an easy mathematical step that comes next.

The "R" value is the *resistance* to heat

passage through the material and is the *reciprocal* of the C value. To get it you simply place the figure 1 over the C value, making it into a fraction. Thus if the material has a C value of 4 (meaning it loses 4 Btu's per hour per square foot, per degree of temperature difference) it has an R value of ¼. For easy figuring, you change it to a decimal, here .25. This is the form of R value you find on the labels of insulation packages. You might find a figure like R-24 (a worthwhile value) on 6″ thick fiberglass you'd use to insulate between joists in your attic. Or it might be R-11 to fit in the walls.

To find out how much heat you're losing through an area of your house shell, like a wall, you add up all the R values of the wall materials. Even the film of air next to the inside and outside wall surfaces has an insulating value. (The outside surface is usually figured on the basis of a 15 M.P.H. wind.) If you start with a typical non-winterized cottage wall without any insulation, it might add up like this:

Inside surface (air)	.68
Gypsum wallboard (½″)	.45
Airspace inside wall	.97
Plywood sheathing (⅜″)	.47
Wood siding (like clapboard)	.98
Outside wall surface (air)	.17
	3.72

The 3.72 is the total resistance to heat passage. To find out how much heat leaks through each square foot of the wall for each degree of inside-outside temperature difference, you convert the figure to its reciprocal, again by placing the figure 1 above it (dividing 3.72 into 1). This shows you are losing about .27 Btu's per square foot for each degree.

Assuming a typical wall area of 1,400 square feet, the 1 degree heat loss comes to 378 Btu's per hour. If you also assume a typical winter temperature difference of 50 degrees, however, the loss climbs to 18,900 Btu's lost each hour through the wall area. But if you replace the air space inside the wall with a layer of R-7 insulation you increase your resistance per square foot from 3.72 to 9.75. Converting to the reciprocal again, you find you're now losing only about .1 Btu per square foot where you were losing .27 before. Multiply it out for 1,400 square feet at a 50 degree temperature difference and you're losing only 7,000 Btu's per hour instead of 18,900. So you're saving 11,900 Btu's every hour. Multiply that by 24 hours and you're saving 285,600 Btu's every day. That's the amount of heat in more than 2 gallons of fuel oil, more than 285 cubic feet of gas, or 83 kilowatts of electricity. Just check on the price of the fuel you're using, add up the days in a heating season and keep it in mind when you think about insulation. And don't forget the weather-stripping.

There are, of course, other factors involved, including the efficiency of your heating equipment. But ample insulation means money in your pocket. If your house has the best possible insulation, you can use the methods outlined to see just how much you've been saving over the years.

ADD INSULATION IN AN ATTIC

If you'd like to add insulation to an existing house there are a few easy ways to do it. The easiest, of course, is in an unfinished attic where you can simply pour

Fig. 159. The R-7 on this roll of Fiberglas insulation tells you the relative insulating power, as described in the text.

Fig. 160. Fiberglass with aluminum on one surface can be used when you're insulating an open wall, as in an unfinished attached garage. The aluminum goes toward the inside. If wallboard is to go over it, the aluminum should be ¾" from the wallboard to have proper reflective effect.

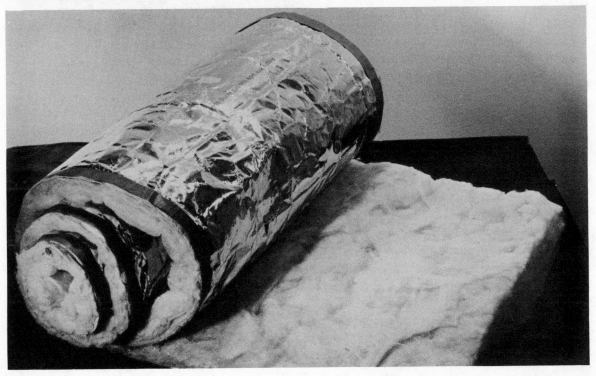

some types of granular or pellet type insulation between the joists that support the ceiling below (if there's no attic floor) and then rake the insulation surface level at the depth you want it. Or you can buy fiberglass insulation that fits snugly between conventionally spaced joists and just push it in place. All you need is a sheet of plywood that you can slide around over the joists to act as a temporary floor area from which you can do the work. But there's a good chance that the attic has already been insulated in one of these ways, either by you or a previous owner. If it's skimpy, however, you can add another layer. To further increase the insulating ability of your house you'll usually have to re-insulate in other areas.

YOU CAN HAVE IT BLOWN INTO WALLS

If you look through the Yellow Pages of your local phone book (or nearby ones, if you live in an outlying area) under "Insulation" you'll usually find insulating firms that can blow insulation into the outside walls of your house. This is possible if you know the walls contain no insulation. It's done by boring holes through the outer wall surface (between the supporting studs in the wall) and blowing the insulation in with special equipment. The price of the job is usually based on the square footage of wall into which the insulation is blown.

Usually, a few shingles or clapboards are removed so the holes can be bored through the sheathing beneath. Then, after the insulation is blown in, the holes are plugged and the shingles or clapboards replaced. So the house exterior looks just as

it did before the job. As the entire air space inside the wall is filled with insulation by this method, you can usually expect a sizable improvement in insulating value.

OR ADD PANELS OF POLYSTYRENE FOAM

If you'd like a method of adding insulation to an existing house without hiring outside help, you can use panels of insulating polystyrene foam. These come in several forms, some with tongued and grooved edges that fit together like flooring boards, others in simple 2x4' rectangular panels. The panels, as an example, are readily available in 1" thickness with an R value (resistance) of 4. They're also available on order in 2" thickness with an R value of 8. Approximately the same thicknesses and R values are available in other forms of the material. Check them with your local code.

Using a special mastic, made for use with the foam, you can stick the panels to your inside walls and top floor ceilings. As the panel forms are widely used in dropped ceilings, they're a clear white with an attractive surface texture that requires no painting. If they are used on walls, however, they should be covered by a layer of gypsum board as they're relatively soft and subject to impact damage. Before you plan on this type of insulation, check on its burning characteristics and on the methods of installation recommended by the manufacturer. Typical panel forms will burn if flame is directed against them but will not continue to burn after the flame is removed. Covered by a layer of gypsum board, of course, they're protected.

If you do an interior foam insulating

job, however, you'll have to plan for the trim around windows and doorways. Often the simplest way to handle this aspect of the work is by adding trim to that already there and overlapping it slightly onto the new wall surface. The insulation need be applied only to outside walls, of course, so

in most cases, you'll reduce the overall room size by only about 1½". And you can do the job a room at a time. Think about it. And add up the R values of your present insulation plus the R value of the foam you'd use. And check your local code.

Fig. 161. Foam type insulation. Top is expanded polystyrene with aluminum on one surface for reflective effect. Below it, foam with waterproof coating on one surface. Next, plain polystyrene foam. All these in 1" thickness. Bottom, expanded polystyrene foam in 2" thickness.

Fig. 162. If you insulate ceiling directly under roof, as in an enclosed porch, you can use dropped ceiling methods and use wood or hardboard grilles under the foam for decorative effect, like this.

Fig. 163. Handy tools for insulating from the inside wall inward. Left to right: Folding rule, for measuring and outlining foam. Putty knife for applying mastic. Old all stainless steel table knife for cutting foam, stapler for installing fiberglass, and large scissors for cutting fiberglass. The table knife is heated by the propane torch (top of photo) then held in pot holder to protect hands while cutting. The heated knife cuts the expanded polystyrene foam as if it were butter and smoothseals the cut edge. Do not bring knife to red heat.

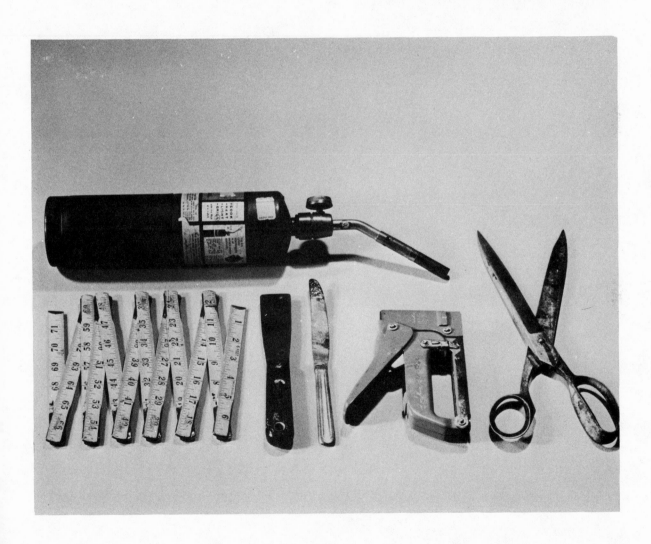

APPENDIX II

WHERE TO BUY IT ALL

It's seldom difficult to find a source of wood stoves, factory-made fireplaces and chimneys and the accessories that go with them. If you live in a fair-sized town the chances are you can buy them all locally from hardware or building supply dealers. Many lumberyards also stock them. As major mail order houses also handle these items, they may be your best bet in outlying areas. You can make your selection from the illustrations and specifications in the catalogs. (If you're looking for a wood stove, however, you'll usually find it listed in the index under "heaters, wood.")

As for masonry supplies, you can usually find sources in your local phone book's Yellow Pages under mason contractors' equipment and supplies. It's worthwhile visiting one of these outlets before you decide on your overall styling of a masonry fireplace. You may find unusual types of block or stone that you'd like to incorporate in the work.

When you shop for accessories like andirons or fire tongs you may also find devices intended to increase the heating efficiency of your fireplace, if it is not a circulating type. These range from hollow, tubular grates that emit warmed air into the room from their forward-leaning upper ends, to more elaborate blower-assisted types. Their efficiency varies with their design. Safety is the important point.

If you want a particular type of equipment that's shown or described in this book and identified by name, look for it in the address list that follows, and write the manufacturer for prices and details.

Albert Constantine and Son, Inc.
2050 Eastchester Road
Bronx, New York 10461
(Moldings for fireplace fronts)

Ashley Automatic Heater Company
Division of Martin Industries, Inc.
1604 17th Avenue, S.W.
P.O. Box 730
Sheffield, Alabama 35660
(Ashley wood stoves)

Brookfield Fireside El-Fuego
Route 7
Brookfield, Connecticut 06804
(El-Fuego in-fireplace heaters)

C & D Distributors
   P.O. Box 715
   Old Saybrook, Connecticut 06478
   (Wood stoves)

Heatilator Fireplaces
   Division of Vega Industries
   Mt. Pleasant, Iowa 52641
   *(Heatilator factory-made circulating
   fireplaces)*

Hart & Cooley Mfg. Co.
   Division of Allied Thermal Corp.
   Holland, Michigan 49423
   (Metlvent factory-made chimneys)

The Majestic Company
   Huntington, Indiana 46750
   *(Majestic factory-made fireplaces
   and chimneys)*

Owens/Corning Fiberglas Corp.
   Home Building Products Division
   Toledo, Ohio 43601
   (Fiberglass insulation)

Portland Cement Association
   33 West Grand Avenue
   Chicago, Illinois 60610
   (Cement)

Portland Stove Foundry, Inc.
   57 Kennebec Street
   Portland, Maine 04104
   (Cast-iron wood stoves)

Portland Willamette Co.
   6805 N.E. 59th Place
   Portland, Oregon 97218
   (Fireplace accessories)

Preston Distributing Company
   Whidden Street
   Lowell, Massachusetts 01852
   (King and Chapée French stoves)

Riteway Mfg. Co.
   Marco Industries
   Division of Sarco Corporation
   P.O. Box 6
   Harrisonburg, Virginia 22801
   (Automatic wood burners)

Sears Roebuck and Co.
   Contact catalog office nearest you as
   listed in your local phone directory
   *(Cast-iron wood stoves, fireplaces
   and accessories)*

Templet Industries Incorporated
   201 East Bethpage Road
   Plainview, New York 11803
   (Templet wood stoves)

United States Mineral Products Company
   Stanhope, New Jersey 17874
   (Foam-type insulation)

Wilton Stove Works
   P.O. Box 216
   Bethlehem, Connecticut 06751
   (Wood stoves)

INDEX

Plumbing, 80, 82
Poker, 146
Polystyrene foam insulating panels, 180-182
Portland Cement Association, 67, 68, 72, 138, 186
Portland Stove Foundry, Inc., 186;
  fireplaces by, *23, 151;*
  stoves by, *22, 114, 149, 150, 154*
Portland Willamette Company, 186;
  screens and accessories by, *135, 142-147*
Potbelly stove, 26, *27,* 32, 113, 148, *149;*
  chimney for, 75, *97*
Preston Distributing Company, 150, 186

R valve, 177-181
Raccoons, 167, 173
Radiant heat, 13, 19, 21, 113
Radiant stoves, 113, *114*
Radiators (hot air registers), 162
Rain shield, 97
Reflected heat, 17, 21
Roof, chimney and, 39, 59, 64, 91-98, 105-107;
  and factory-made chimney, 77, 98;
  flashing, 95-97; termination, 106
Room-divider fireplace, *136*
Room heaters; *See* Wood stoves
Rumford, Count, 17-19

Safety factors, 113-116
Sand, 32;
  in mortar mix, 40
Savot, Dr. Louis, 16
Scaffolding, 61
Sears, Roebuck and Company, 150, 186;
  Wonder Wood automatic stove by, *114*
Seasoning firewood, 160
Secondary air, 26, 30
Sheet metal wall protection, 115, 116
Smoke, 24;
  from fireless fireplace, 168-169;
  from fireplace, 49, 54, 55, 165-173;
  from wood stove, 31, 32, 173-174;
  problem in early fireplaces, 9, 11, 13, 15
Smoke chamber, 51-54; 71
Smoke louvre, 9, *12*

Smoke pipe, 27, 173-174
Smoke shelf, 17, 18, 49, 172
Smoke test, 62
Smoke vent, 9
Soda bread recipe, 19
Soot, 77, 172; pocket, *87,* 173-174
Spark arrester, 167, 172-173
Squirrels, 167, 173
Storm collar, *95, 96*
Stove; *See* Franklin stove; In-the-fireplace
  stove; Wood stove
Stovepipe, 84, 115, 173
Stud location, 80

Tailwind, 15, 16
Taut string alignment, 40, 41
Television antenna, 65
Templet Industries, Inc., 186;
  Sherwood fireplace, *122*
Textured materials, 136-137
Thermagard insulation, 76
Thermo-siphoning, 76-78, 80, 98, 104, 106
Thermostat, 30, 114, 162-163
Tongs, 146
Tools, for fireplace, *142, 143,* 145-147;
  for insulating walls, *183*

Vapors, 29, 31, 32
Ventilation, 17, 169

Wall fireplace, 13, *15*
Walls, stove distance from, 113-117
Washtub (for wood), 161-162
Weather-stripping, 178
Wet wood (logs), 145, 159, 161
Wilton Stove Works, 186;
  stoves by, 29, *137, 152*
Wind problems, 170-172;
  See also Downdraft
Wire mesh, 173-174
Wiring, house, 82
Wood; *See* Firewood
Wood framing, 62, 64

Wood stove, 17, 19, 21, 77, 148-154;
    automatic, 30;
    factory-made chimney for, 77, 80;
    fireplace stoves, 115, 118-122, 148-154;
    heat from, 157, 162-163;
    how it works, 26;
    how to buy and install, 113-125;
    how to start a fire in, 30-32;
    smoke problems, 173-174;

    space and safety factors, 113-115;
    types, *27-30,* 113-114;
    where to buy, 185-186
Woodpile, *158,* 161-162

Zero clearance, 102-105, 108
Zoned heating system, 162